W9-BWI-337

HEIRESS OF ALL THE AGES

♀

♀

Heiress of all the ages

♀

♀ *Sex and sentiment*

♀ *in the genteel tradition*

by WILLIAM WASSERSTROM

THE UNIVERSITY OF MINNESOTA PRESS
Minneapolis

Library of Congress Catalog Card Number: 59-7949

Published in Great Britain, India, and Pakistan by the Oxford University Press, London, Bombay, and Karachi and in Canada by Thomas Allen, Ltd., Toronto

IN MEMORY OF

Isaiah Wasserstrom

Nellie Wasserstrom

Preface

I HAVE WRITTEN AN ESSAY that undertakes to study the genteel tradition, its place in American social history, its effect on literature. Referring to a cluster of ideas, expectations, methods, and values common in the age of gentility, I have tried to connect the public life of society with the private life of imagination.

The common view of the genteel tradition is of a period of years in the American past beginning, let us say, in the 1830's and ending with the First World War. Actually, traces appear earlier and the climax occurs sooner but it is full-fledged during those eighty-odd years. Ordinarily, the tradition is noted for its adherence to the twin principles of manliness and womanliness. Rooted in the eighteenth-century idea about natural nobility, manliness signified a state of the soul which negated the claims of the body; womanliness resulted when the body was eliminated. Gentlemen were manly, ladies were womanly. And in literature, women rather than men seemed best suited to preach this morality. Choosing certain real young women as its model, polite fiction praised their beauty, their wit, their innocence, their virtue. Young ladies appeared in numerous stories that present neat lessons and nice amusements. Life was cozy, threatened only by occasional badness in the great world. Then after the Civil War, lives were threatened by general badness, even in literature, and especially in the writing of a man who stood outside his tradition, Henry James. By 1910 ladies and gentlemen lamented the loss of a golden age. And by 1920 that age had turned to brass.

But this is an inadequate image of the past. For the really surprising thing is that, despite itself, a caste-minded, money-minded society, confused by liberty, awed by sex, and sentimental about love, produced a unique literature. It was guided by a moral vision which integrated and unified its three leading preoccupations—sex, love, and freedom.

At the beginning of the last century America was a struggling republic with high hopes and vague boundaries. By 1900 society had acquired specific borders and a national character. During the intervening hundred years, numerous influences, disruptive and unifying, foreign and domestic, had helped to mold American life: some of its hopes had been fulfilled, others had been overlooked, still others had been turned into malign instruments of power. During the whole time of its transformation, however, society was sustained by a certain sense of its destiny. The American dream of justice and freedom for all men may have been degraded, but the dream itself provided a discipline, a group of values, which everyone shared.

For it was not until the First World War that Americans lost their sense of destiny; not till then did life become too complicated to be explained according to the principle Hegel had asserted in the *Philosophy of History* and Turner had traced to the influence of the frontier. In the New World, Hegel said, a nation was finally established in which mankind was to be allowed to make good its claim to dignity. America would allow man to develop all his capacities, encourage him to fulfill himself. The history of civilization, as Europe illustrated, was a record of human ineptitude. The American experience would contradict and rewrite history for it would dramatize the oldest of all truths: free men alone know the true meaning of love. Only they, therefore, can live in harmony.

But historic contradictions could be resolved and legendary dreams fulfilled only when certain dilemmas, inherent in society and in the inner lives of all its members, were exposed, recognized, resolved. The oldest of all antitheses had been transported here in the minds of the people who settled the Massachusetts Bay Colony. Children of light, according to their own Manichean view of the nature of things, they saw confronting them the Indian children of darkness. And when some of their neighbors undertook to remold life according to the pagan model, at Merrymount, these heretics were expelled from the community. Later, in the eighteenth century, when one of their own number, Jonathan Edwards, tried to redirect their attention to its proper field of study, to the claims of the invisible world, it was he who was expelled by congregations that enjoyed studying God through Franklin's microscope. It is the conflict between these two modes of attention which shapes the American character, Van Wyck Brooks said nearly forty-five years ago — at nearly the same moment when Fitzgerald decided that he was a cross between St. Francis of Assisi and J. P. Morgan. Recently, too, Richard Chase, in his *The American Novel and Its Tradition,* has contended that unresolved tensions of exactly this kind shape the essential character of our whole literature. As, let us say, Emerson's mind is the field of battle in which two forces forever conflict, freedom and fate, so our literature portrays the field itself, the battle, and the eternal postponement of victory. Mr. Chase argues that American writing is in fact distinguished precisely because it pictures human life as a drama of contradictions which, for better or worse, remain unresolved and untranscended.

It would be odd indeed if a dualism which flourishes in all spheres of American letters and culture were excluded from the matter of love. For it is in the literature of love that we retrace the center of motive and recover the origins of attitude. It is there that we uncover cross-purposes if these do in fact exist; there, too, we discover what irreconcilable impulses lead to which forms of imbalance and balance.

To my mind, the overriding aim even of genteel fiction — which is very deeply grounded in, yet *transcends,* moral dualism — is to establish order within the human spirit and in the life of society. What began as an effort to compose sentimental, polite entertainments culminated in a complex literature which portrayed the unity of love and the interrelatedness of love and freedom. Whitman's opinion — "the soul is not more than the body" and "the body is not more than the soul"; "if anything is sacred the human body is sacred"—is prefigured, not unique but common, not eccentric to the genteel tradition but its very core. It supported a popular literature which, like Whitman's poetry, recognized that society could not competently fulfill its great tasks if men and women were themselves distraught, rendered incompetent to love. Vast distances of wilderness, religious disorganization, political disorder, slavery, Civil War, tenements, strikes—all these problems will be overcome, our literature says, when men and women resolve the dilemmas of love. Only then will society fulfill the dream of history. This dream was best symbolized in the American girl, Henry James believed, and if this society is the heir of all the ages, she is the heiress. It became therefore her duty to resolve and transcend all antitheses. When she failed, the result in literature was tragic. But when she brought off the victory, she paid the nation's debt to history and thereby performed the solemn, heroic office of the heiress of all the ages.

I am grateful to the University of Rochester for grants-in-aid which helped to make certain problems less troublesome. I'm grateful also to the editors of those journals—*The American Imago*, the *American Quarterly*, *ELH*, *A Journal of English Literary History*—in which some of this material has appeared. Earlier versions of this study itself were substantially improved as a result of comment and criticism by Jacques Barzun, Richard Hofstadter, F. W. Dupee, Richard Chase, and Lionel Trilling. I have come to recognize, too, my special debt to Lionel Trilling for he has helped me to assume the duties of a teacher and critic of literature.

What is hardest to foresee is the way a project of this sort takes over your home. Your wife tries, gently, to say that this or that phrase is stuffy, unconvincing; to be patient when you decide to change something in her supposedly clean copy. And she tries even harder to undo your effect on young sons who set up a grocer's shop that sells milk, bread, and footnotes. In certain essential ways this book is a product of collaboration and I am profoundly indebted to Rose.

W. W.

♀

Contents

HEIRESS OF ALL THE AGES

♀

Steel-engraving ladies and Gibson girls

"The Victorians gazed upon the world with innocent eyes, unclouded with our modern sense of guilt, our incomprehension and our inadequacy. And if we feel, as we read them, that they were a little like babes in the woods, at least they were cheerful babes and they possessed the singular advantage of knowing where they thought they were going."

"THERE IS NO DOUBT," Oscar Wilde in 1882 told his American audiences, "that within a century from now the whole culture of the New World will be in petticoats."[1] The men and women he addressed accepted this fact and interpreted it as another sign that America was the chosen land, another sign of grace. For Wilde's remarks as well as his visit itself were merely common incidents in a series that had begun a century earlier. Europeans, arriving here and presenting their opinions on manners, morals, and women in America, usually announced that American women were not only more impressive than men but also were livelier, handsomer, brighter, more deft, more adaptable, and more virtuous than women elsewhere. "No country," said the English ambassador, Lord Bryce, "seems to owe more to its women, nor to owe them so much of what is best in social institutions."[2] Wilde's remark may have disguised a sneer but it was on the surface a compliment of the most usual kind.

In literature, the chief result of this mystique of sex — women are better than men — is a preference for heroines rather than heroes. These girls were designed to represent the whole range of attitudes and ideals, achievements and failures, that defined civilization in the United States. They embodied its morals, argued its politics, symbolized its aspirations. The explanation of the heroine's place in the American imagination which Santayana suggested,

Howells and Van Wyck Brooks approved, sees this as an effect of the general feminization of culture. If you were a proper editor, says Thomas Beer, a spokesman for this view, "bred in the society of Newark or Hartford, you did not trifle with the Titaness and for her sake you issued tales of women, by women, for women." [3]

This opinion, however, does not account for the ways this audience achieved power. It does not say why American society acceded to the principles laid down, at mid-century, in the Ohio Female Convention: American women are superior to men "in religion, in taste, in general elevation of sentiment and in consistency of standard opinions." [4] But our culture and our literature are not merely the products of female vanity. Rather, vanity and the prime role of women in fiction occur because first, the rationale of American life encouraged women to strike for freedom and forced men to support their effort; second, society was dissatisfied with its sexual customs and initiated an inquiry into the whole matter which continues today; third, our women themselves, reared under new conditions and aided by the world-wide feminist movement, simply became more impressive than earlier civilization had permitted women to be.

The history of the elaborate literature inspired by these women begins in 1800 when a girl held many of the same attitudes that marked people of her class in Europe. The chances are slight that she had read Mary Wollstonecraft's scandalous book on women's rights; but if she had she probably agreed with her father and brothers that its views applied only to European girls, who were ignorant and frivolous anyway, given to drinking chocolate in bed after eleven, bred to be amiable bedfellows of men of fashion. On the contrary, American girls were bred with a high sense of duty: their first duty in the land where Everygirl was queen was to provide a grateful people many healthy princes. "It is said that when the Duke of Orleans made his formal *demande* for the hand of [Mr. Willing's] . . . daughter, [the father replied] . . . 'Should you ever be restored to your hereditary position you will be too great a match for her; if not, she is too great a match for you.'" [5] Nearly three quarters of a century later, when the American experiment had taken certain unforeseen shifts, Whitman was to urge—"I promulge a new race of Teachers, of Perfect Women . . . to endow the birth-stock of a New World"—a return to this basic dignity of democracy. In 1800, girls were told to attend not Miss Wollstonecraft but Hannah More. She urged women to respect themselves and woman's work, avoid encroaching upon masculine interests or entering the theater of masculine activity. Harriet Martineau observed that Mrs. More's works were better known in America than the plays of Shakespeare.

During the first quarter of the century, therefore, women did not feel that social restraint was a conspiracy of men who wished to preserve for themselves the pleasures of the world. Tocqueville, for example, noticed that though there were two distinct lines of action for the sexes, American society forced each to keep pace with the other. Public education had been available to girls in New England since the middle of the eighteenth century. They were permitted to attend the same schools where boys were taught, but they went only for short periods and after the boys had been dismissed. They were taught reading, writing, arithmetic, and religion. In addition, the daughter of a well-to-do family in 1815 "sings, dances, plays on the lute and harpsichord, paints prettily, is a perfect mistress of the French tongue, and has made considerable progress in Italian. She is, besides, excellently skilled in all domestic sciences." [6] This is the person whom Frances Wright admired and described in her letters home to England: "the freedom of national manners" encourages this girl to do her chores with "sweetness, artlessness, and liveliness." "These laughing creatures," Miss Wright reported, move and speak "with a grace that art never taught." [7]

During these years, therefore, women were reared according to a discipline that mixed old and new elements. Their main duty, however, was to adorn their husband's crown and as yet their effect upon society was small. American men are proud of their women, Captain Marryat observed, "flatter them, are kind to them," but in fact the women themselves "have at present no influence whatever in society." [8] "It is in vain," Mrs. Trollope sneered, "that 'collegiate institutes' are founded for young ladies, or that 'academic degrees' are conferred upon them." It is after marriage that the "lamentable insignificance of American women appears." [9] America encouraged no salons in which — traditionally — bright, gifted, and bored women achieved power by indirectly influencing the maneuvers of empire. Indeed, Europeans complained that conversation here consisted of female talk for the women, politics for the men, spiced by the abominable national pastime of spitting and varied only by card games. Society had been given over to the "unmarried young," though a little later we hear that it included the festivities of the boarding house — "filled with celibates who are not always monks or nuns." [10] By mid-century a leisured middle class had been created which faced a new problem: how may leisure be joyfully used?

Apparently, these people did not know quite what to do with themselves and when they fashioned their clothes and manners upon the European model, they were warned that they violated the national spirit. "The women of the higher classes in Europe alone enjoy the privileges of ease which are so universally vouchsafed to the female sex in America." An upper-class woman in France or England is bred for a life of leisure and has "resources for interest and occupation in the traditional social duties which are attached to her inheritance." American girls wear elaborate clothing simply to exchange calls during which they merely gossip about their servants or one another. They endanger themselves and, in marriage, their families because they feel that "unhealthy sensual excitement" of the European life of fashion without knowing also its "wholesome intellectual relief." This writer, indeed, defines the situation which today we describe as the dilemma of modern women: "the fine ladies," he says, ought not to be thrust "back among the pots and kettles." Nonetheless, "a daily interest in the routines of household duty would improve their health and not spoil their beauty." [11] Unfortunately, these routines often included a large awkward house, difficult servants, frightening and unfamiliar children, and a husband who spent very little time at home. Women who had leisure, intelligence, vivacity, were well-equipped to protest; and by the 1840's, therefore, the crusade for "rights" was at hand. The New American Woman began to fancy herself as a New Woman.

Men tried to discourage these intrusive people by saying that they ought not to remove themselves from The Home, their proper domain. A woman was after all a "purer, brighter being, an emanation of some better world, irradiating like a rainbow the stormy elements of life." [12] But the time was past when rhetoric could replace rights. If we are as impressive as all that, they argued, give us better education, actual legal existence, social power rather than the so-called empire of the heart. They simply turned the idea upside down. And in order to bolster their argument they reminded society how powerfully women had upheld moral principles when, in Washington, men of station and reputation had capitulated to Jackson's mob. For it was an incontrovertible fact that, during the years between 1829 and 1837, when the spoilsmen corrupted the Jeffersonian tradition, ladies had taken a stand against social, political, and moral evil. They chose as its symbol Peggy Eaton, née O'Neill, Jackson's particular friend, the ex-wife of a naval purser who had committed suicide; she had been the mistress and later became the wife of Secretary of War Eaton. "The President . . . actually held a cabinet meeting about Mrs. Eaton, where he pronounced her 'chaste as a virgin,'" [13] but Washington society ladies refused to call or even to speak. This led to a first-rate scandal and caused Jackson to think that he was being undermined by the aristocrats in his party. But best of all, it demonstrated that women were able to assert the claim of decency, even of prudery, in the great world where men were inclined to measure advantages, not morals.

The field of activity to which women were first attracted was, quite sensibly, education. In 1821 Emma Willard had opened her Troy Seminary in order to give women an education similar to that offered in the men's universities. Then in 1823 and 1829 the Hartford Female Academy and the Abbott Academy for Girls were established—institutes to which Mrs. Trollope referred. But before the middle classes would support these schools a case had to be made for the value of an education for girls. The editor of

Godey's, Sarah Josepha Hale, formulated the line of thought mirrored in most of the ladies' magazines: in 1830 she wrote about the importance of education and then in "the 1840's and 1850's she campaigned for high schools for girls. In the 1850's and 1860's, federally supported schools and colleges for women" were included in her campaign. The women she spoke for built their case on the need for more teachers in a society that planned to provide universal free elementary education. "There must be more teachers," they argued, "but the wages that the individual teacher received must be lower. At a time when a farm awaited almost any man and growing industry offered countless opportunities, such a supply of teachers could be recruited only among girls and women." [14] Doubtless this argument suited women who were trying very hard to establish their place in a male profession but unfortunately their eagerness to sacrifice money for career became, in the popular American mind, the leading motive of people who teach.[15]

The overriding reason why women were established as teachers is that they used with great effect the legend of feminine superiority. "Women were better teachers for young children than men" because their "moral influence" was far superior. "If there is one word in the English language dearer than all others, it is that of Ma . . . It is our Ma who directs the tiny feet in their first struggles; it is our Ma who teaches the prattling tongue . . . and it is our Ma . . . who through all the stages of youth implants within us the purer thoughts and stronger principles of an honest life." "What is home without a Ma?" [16] And women asked, in turn, what is a school without a schoolmarm? If men believed that American women were divine then surely the only sensible thing for them to do was to put these glorious people into the schoolrooms.

The growth of an urgent and fatuous sentimentality in American life substantially aided ambitious women to increase their influence in society. But it was the feminist movement itself that gave coherence to their effort. Initially feminism had been identified with the movement to abolish Negro slavery, a condition comparable to theirs, many women held. A familiar story tells how in 1834 male abolitionists refused women the right to join their organization; the women then formed a group of their own against great opposition: in 1838 a Philadelphia mob burned the hall in which they were meeting. And two years later the World Anti-Slavery Convention refused to seat American women delegates. In consequence, Lucretia Mott and Elizabeth Cady Stanton returned here and launched a formal woman's rights movement which by 1845 so impressed the Scandinavian novelist Frederika Bremer, then visiting America and talking over problems with feminist leaders here, that she returned to Sweden and wrote *Hertha*, a novel which encouraged Swedish women to follow the American example. And by 1848 the movement had achieved sufficient force to warrant publication of a Declaration of Sentiments based upon the Declaration of Independence. Society was therefore ready, at the beginning of the fifties, for the Ohio Female Convention which, as we have remarked, proclaimed as an irrefragible fact of life the physical, intellectual, moral, and doctrinal superiority of American women.

Obviously, women had come a considerable distance in a single generation. Suddenly, society became aware that its traditional procedures and idolatries were under pressure and in the late fifties the lines of battle were drawn. Assertive women and their male supporters urged a still more vigorous effort which would finally establish a woman's right to choose how she would live. They were opposed by men and women who believed that such thoughts were unladylike, profane. "The True Heroine" has "never had a selfish thought," is "wondrous gentle" in a sickroom, has taught her children to be "pure and true and brave and strong and courteous" so that "*Home* was their treasure and their pride." An increasing number of women argued, however, that "Some of us have hearts and minds. So much the worse for us and you." "We have been told," traditionalists returned, "how many spirits among women are of a wider, stronger heroic mold than befits the mere routine of housekeeping . . . Where is the woman any way too great, or too high, or too wise, to spend herself in creating a home?" But by 1860 so bald an attempt to shame women into a proper respect for their "functions" seemed mere bombast. "We should be very grateful,

Sir / That when you've nothing else to do / You waste your idle hours on us / So kind of you!"[17] Genteel ladies and gentlemen reminded their critics that for reasons of health alone girls in America were disqualified from participating in affairs outside their homes: "The American girl is a very delicate plant . . . more exquisitely organized than the English or German girl," and though she is "more self-relying than the Italian or French, yet not generally strong in nerve or muscle."[18] Feminists replied that girls in Lowell, Massachusetts, had been operating the mills effectively since 1822. But their argument was unconvincing because it was common knowledge that physical and emotional energy declined in proportion to rank and breeding. Even in England, where women were healthier, it had been found that "the proportion of women who can suckle their children is decidedly diminishing among the upper and middle classes, that deaths from childbirth are eight times as great . . . and that spinal distortion, hysteria, and painful disorders are on the increase."[19] What is the use, therefore, of founding "colleges for girls whom even the high school breaks down . . . How appeal to any woman to enlarge her thoughts beyond the mere drudgery of the household when she 'dies daily' beneath the exhaustion of even that?"[20] This line of thought was disingenuous because women were discouraged from improving their health: "walking in the streets of New York accompanied by their husbands and their brothers," ladies of "irreproachable character" described how they were "hissed and hooted" and had "the most insulting words addressed to them" merely because they wore the "bloomer dress."[21] Of course these women had been unable to comprehend the effect of their dress upon the male sexual imagination in which it figured not as a shift from illness toward health but as challenge and rivalry.

The feminist controversy, which began shortly before the Civil War, continued at least until 1918 when women, finally allowed to vote, lost the best symbol of dissension. Before the argument ended, however, very serious charges were made on both sides. Manly men and womanly women were committed to an ideal of marriage in which the woman painfully submitted to her husband's demands. Her first duty was to be a "Ma" and she was supposed to be impelled by the divine instinct of motherhood. But it was public knowledge that somehow she did not look "seriously enough upon the magnificent function of maternity." After marriage, many gentlemen discovered that their wives were not only the victims of countless illnesses but also they seemed chronically discontented with their incomes, their homes. In "Every Wife Her Own Tormentor," for example, the husband is pictured arriving at his door, resigned and sad: "Lingering, he raised the latch at eve / Though tired in heart and limb / He loved no other place, and yet / Home was no home for him."[22] This was particularly discomfiting because a man's wife assured his salvation. She was supposed to be in communion with God, praying that her sexual martyrdom would achieve for her husband eternal grace. Renewed in heaven, he would come to her disembodied but grateful. According to this discipline, unmarried men were "in imminent personal danger" for only with a wife does a man possess the "sense of being protected from the . . . temptations of the world." "Said a strong man to us once, 'When I am near my wife and children all the hells seem shut . . . and the devils are out of sight; but when they are out of town, a whole legion of devils seem barking at once.' "[23] This situation, in our day, is known as *The Seven Year Itch.*

A true, noble woman was guided by something called the Eternal Feminine which yearned "to integrate itself in the companionship" with something else called the Secular Manly, a companionship "that is strongest and most blessed after the passions have ceased to heat the blood."[24] But this ideal hardly sustained the tired man who was afraid to open the door to his house. If his wife had had an especially difficult day—"the nervous petulance of wives may be named among the sources of domestic discomfort and alienation"—he required all the manliness he could muster. For when an American lady's natural strength "is perverted," she becomes "the petulant tyrant, the terrible shrew of the household, with a tongue set on fires of hell."[25] The domestic situation which genteel ladies and gentlemen wished to perpetuate, therefore, did not quite conform to the public ideal. The following poem embodies the manners of the day as well as the bicker and anxiety which manners masked. At first glance it is an encomium of the usual sort but it is arranged so that its thought will transpire only when its lines are read properly. You read lines 1 and 3, then 2 and 4, and supply all suitable punctuation.

That man must lead a happy life
Who is directed by a wife.
Who's freed from matrimonial claims
Is sure to suffer for his pains.

Adam could find no solid peace
'Til he beheld a woman's face;
When Eve was given for a mate
Adam was in a happy state.

In all the female race appear
Truth, darling of a heart sincere,
Hypocrisy, deceit, and pride
In woman never did reside.

What tongue is able to unfold
The worth in woman we behold?
The failings that in woman dwell
Are almost imperceptible.

Confusion take the men, I say
Who no regard to women pay.
Who make the women their delight,
Keep always reason in their sight.[26]

We must drop, therefore, the clichés which ordinarily describe love in the age of confidence and we must modify our image of leisured, bright women, devoted to the arts, pleading for more sympathy from men immersed in business. Indeed, the ideal of love which genteel ladies spoke for and which they protected against the attack of New Women, was unconvincing on still another ground. "Three out of every four married women," we are told in 1882 by the reviewer of a book called *Effect on Woman of Imperfect Hygiene of the Sexual Function*, "suffer from sexual ill-health due to ignorance before and after marriage." "Girls utterly fail to connect their erotic sensations with the reproductive organs." The main result of this ignorance — which the womanly women hoped to preserve — was "no definite disease, but only a general feeling of debility." These remarks occur fairly early in the controversy but their substance became increasingly public. The sexual revolution which was to occur forty years later, however, is foreshadowed in this writer's insistence that "If your sexual life be pure and healthy, you are every whit whole."[27] This striking doctrine was violently opposed, of course, by women who relied upon the advice given in *Dr. Chase's Recipes* — a medical handbook which, by 1867, had gone through forty-six editions. There women were taught that what the psychiatrist S. Weir Mitchell was to call the domestic demon, feminine hysteria, resulted from novels that "excite sexual thoughts," so Dr. Chase believed; from "sedentary habits, stimulating food, standing out talking with supposed friends (real enemies)" when healthy girls should be "by the fire or in bed"; "masturbation, excessive cohabitation, miscarriages."[28] Another book of this kind warned that the effects of what it called "certain solitary and social vices" were "defective memory . . . dimness of vision, morbid fears . . . paralysis of will."

This particular argument was subsumed within the general controversy but obviously it defined a basic disagreement indeed. Pure women were often hysterically ill, alcoholic, addicted to drugs: "I quietly took opium," says Mrs. Mary Boykin Chestnut.[29] She was the wife of a former Senator who was a senior aide to Jefferson Davis. "It quiets . . . my nerves and I can calmly reason and take rational views of things otherwise maddening."[30] Later, women of this kind took Dr. Mitchell's rest cure. New Women claimed that these disorders resulted from a radical disharmony in sexual relations and did not signify feminine virtue or delicacy. Their views were expressed by a champion of the cause who both pleased and embarrassed them, Victoria Woodhull. This very odd person spent half her life pronouncing the most revolutionary doctrines and the other half denouncing them. She herself, therefore, is a perfect symbol not only of the controversy itself but also of the mood of the time. Before she recanted, however, she gave a series of lectures which set staid society back on its heels. In one of these, "The

Elixir of Life," she said that "intercourse carried on habitually without regard to perfect and reciprocal consummation" is completely immoral and destructive. "I need not explain to any woman the effects of unconsummated intercourse . . . but every man needs to have it thundered in his ears . . . that the other party demands a return for all that he receives, demands that he shall not be enriched at her expense, demands that he shall not, either from ignorance or selfish desire, carry her impulse forward only to cast it backward with its mission unfulfilled, to prostrate the impelling power and breed nervous debility or irritability and sexual demoralization." This condition, she concluded in garbled syntax, has caused "a growing disgust sexually between the sexes." [31] Victoria's opinions were not rejected by the National Woman Suffrage Association. And when certain members objected to the admission into the Association of a person whom the newspapers called the bride of Satan, Miss Elizabeth Cady Stanton defended its decision. She wrote to Lucretia Mott that Victoria "stands before us as an able speaker and writer. Her face, manners and conversation, all indicate the triumph of the moral, intellectual and spiritual." [32] Miss Stanton was either disingenuous or naive — Victoria was a blackmailer and an opportunist — but her statement implies that the Association was not interested merely in establishing a woman's right to vote.

The whole conflict as well as the two feminine archetypes of the later nineteenth century are presented most lucidly in a dialogue called "The Steel-Engraving Lady and the Gibson Girl." It is a conversation between Old and New, between a Lady warmed at the hearth and a Girl who prefers to allow its weak flicker to die. The one dates from the serene time of the golden past when everyone understood that women had a world of their own in which they were supreme. The other is a product of an age of Bessemer furnaces, of workers' strikes and socialist theorizing, of mass immigration and economic depression, moral confusion and sexual assertion. In the Lady's view, the Gibson Girl represents a society tarnished by six years of Grant's corrupt administrations; a society that rejected a reformer, Samuel Tilden, and elected a man who had traded on sectional animosities. She was a living irony. For she represented the society whose "latest style in martyrs," James Russell Lowell said in his ode on Centennial day, was Boss Tweed. Perhaps a better choice than Tweed might have been the American minister to Brazil, J. W. Webb. He defrauded the Brazilian government of $100,000 and fled to Europe; the United States apologized and refunded the money. Lowell might have pointed, too, at Mrs. Astor's stable of four hundred acceptable guests and at her finical and effeminate grooms, Ward McAllister and Harry Lehr. The sweepstakes were held on Fifth Avenue in the fall and winter and in Newport in the spring and summer. The Lady explains to the Gibson Girl that her training had been designed to help her make "home a place of pleasure and inspiration. I was taught grace of motion, drilled in a school of manners . . . In place of your higher education, I had my music and languages and my embroidery frame . . . Your independent views . . . I cannot understand." The Girl, amazed, shrugs and rises: "She surely is an extinct type . . . I must be off. I'm due at the golf links at three-fifteen." "Hail the New Woman—behold she comes apace," the writer concludes, "WOMAN! ONCE MAN'S SUPERIOR NOW HIS EQUAL." [33]

Steel-Engraving Ladies did indeed grow extinct and the literature that recorded their passing became increasingly desperate. Goethe's mysterious universal female principle was invoked, a deep natural force symbolized in Woman. She does not require "rights," for she has duties, heavy and supreme. And those American girls who scramble for prestige and education "have lost the sense of mighty Nature's purpose"; Goethe's "tremendous words . . . '*Das Ewigweibliche zieht uns hinan*'—fall on deaf ears and hardened consciences." [34] This clamor had risen in proportion to the number of girls who, after the Civil War, decided to attend the universities and the new women's colleges. At that time a college education was unusual, yet in 1869, as we know from *Julia Newberry's Diary*, written by a girl of Chicago Society, "Lou Phillips . . . intends going to Vassar College in the fall, the Whitneys are going too." [35] Vassar had just graduated its first class. Smith and Wellesley in 1875, Bryn Mawr in 1885, Mount Holyoke in 1888, Barnard and Radcliffe in 1889 and 1894 established curricula based upon those in the men's universities. By 1880 the girl who has had "a Vassar education and points with pride to her degree," who knows "a Corot from a Boldoni," sets the style for the New American Woman:

> Princes, to you our western breeze
> Bears many a ship and heavy laden.
> What is best we send in these?
> The free and fair young Yankee maiden.[36]

This person, as we know, was finally symbolized as the Gibson Girl, and when Gibson drew his ideal woman, Mark Sullivan says, the world "bowed down in admiration." "That is the typical American girl."[37] This Helen of Troy and Cleopatra of her day, as Sinclair Lewis thought, was the model for girls in New York and Grand Rapids. Debutantes offered themselves as models to Gibson, rooms at Oxford were adorned with his drawings. And by 1900 it was obvious that Ladies were fighting a lost cause. Their opinion of sex, for example, was being replaced by an antithetical view which proclaimed that in the new epoch, "attempts to suppress this emotion . . . can serve only to corrupt the nature of man." Indeed, society came full circle. The leading dogma of the new thought traced to "the sexual emotion" precisely these qualities in humanity and in society which the cult of gentility had claimed for its very own: "the spirit of independence, of individual liberty, intelligence, moral power, beauty . . . social eminence."[38] By 1914, it was possible for a writer to complain about the increase in the number of studies and essays on this subject. Four years earlier, she notes, "it was difficult to find anything to review" but now it was "impossible to review all I could find." And the person who best represented the new order was Gibson's heroine.

Her success provided the world with a lesson in courage and persistence. In her effort to receive a first-rate education, for example, she had outdistanced the women of England who very early had the support of leading public figures. But it was not until the nineties that these people succeeded in establishing at Cheltenham College a place where girls could get training similar to that in the best public schools. At this time, too, Bedford and Girton Colleges were made available to a select few. But public opinion continued to oppose these efforts: in 1847 Tennyson had written "The Princess" in order to mock intellectuality in women and now Gilbert and Sullivan's adaptation of the poem, "Princess Ida"—a love's labors won over the female academy—laughed at feminine pretension. In both countries there was support of education for women but in America support was firmer, more respectable. So impressive a gentleman of taste and learning as the sociologist Lester Ward, for example, argued that women must be better educated because man "has reached a plane of intelligence on which he cares more for intellectual companionship than for the satisfaction of the instinct to reproduce, and unless he can find such companionship in women he will often decline to recruit the race at the expense of his own well-being."[39] It was argued, however, that educated women were refusing to marry men who did not fulfill new high feminine requirements. By 1895 this issue was sufficiently pressing to urge inquiry and that year a study shows that fifty-five per cent of college women were married compared to eighty to ninety per cent of women otherwise educated. The conclusion most widely accepted, however, said that "only half of college women marry . . . Because they come from a special class in which only half of the women marry."[40] Opponents continued to blame feminine "restlessness, wandering purpose, and self-consciousness" upon higher education; even Albert Jay Nock very near our own day believed that "the New Woman of Anglo-American feminism . . . contributed more than her full share to a continuous process of debasement and vulgarisation."[41] Thus virtually every form of social and moral malaise was at one time or another attributed to women who rejected national prejudices. And though we continue to hear complaints about parents who persist in treating a daughter as if she were "only a pretty thing to be petted . . . 'company' for them until she goes to be the Nora of her own 'Doll's House,'"[42] nevertheless by 1910 fifteen thousand girls were students in the women's colleges and twenty thousand in the coeducational schools. The startling fact is that in 1910 "women took 41.5% of the A.B. degrees granted" throughout the country.[43]

Publication of this information was impressive indeed, and inspired European feminists to redouble their effort. The international woman's rights movement had long measured its achievement according to standards set by American women. Originally, the movement itself had occurred in Norway, Finland, and Denmark because women like Frederika Bremer and Aasta Hansteen had returned to Scandinavia from American tours, fired to achieve for European women the kind of freedom common here even in 1850. They received support from men — Bjørnson, Brandes, Ibsen — whose talents were far stronger than the appeal of feminist thought itself. In England in 1889, Ibsen's *A Doll's House* provoked a public discussion similar to that in America. "Was family life so sacred after all? Might not the home itself be a whited sepulchre . . . Were not husbands frequently sensual, inept, and inadequate, and was not a woman's first duty after all to her own self, her sacred ego?" The English girl who was impressed by Nora's courage modeled herself on Gibson's portrait. Suddenly, she seemed remote and proud. A goddess whose dress fell in "stately folds . . . she regarded would-be swains with an air of proud condescension; her voice had a rich drawl of conscious superiority." [44]

In this fashion the American woman's beauty, freedom, wit, candor, and courage symbolized the ideal of women everywhere. Finally, she came to symbolize, in the opinion of European visitors to America near the end of the century, the essence of American democracy itself. In the first decades after 1800, European travelers had come here to discover at first hand how well ancient ideas on democracy had been transformed into new institutions. Then they discovered the miraculous American woman and they — the group included Thérèse Blanc, Jacques Offenbach, Anthony Trollope, Paul Bourget — competed for the most telling adjective, the most convincing vocabulary of love. "What chiefly strikes the stranger," said an Englishman, James Muirhead, is the way an American woman combines "the charm of eternal womanliness with the aroma of a progressive century." He and others were uninterested in nuances of character; they were unaware that this woman embodied a hard-won and incomplete reconciliation of two thoroughly different ideals. What these casual observers saw was "candor, her frankness, her hail-fellow-well-metedness, her apparent absence of consciousness of self or of sex, her spontaneity, her vivacity, her fearlessness."[45] But it was Edith Wharton's friend, the French novelist Paul Bourget, who dazzled everyone when he wrote that an American woman "is like a living object of art, the last fine work of human skill, attesting that the Yankee . . . has been able to draw from this savage world . . . a whole new civilization, incarnated in this woman." To be seen as spontaneously exhibiting the "supreme glory of the spirit," harmoniously ordered so as to provide the effect of a living work of art—this was a new experience for women.[46] And a century of wonder, debate, and anguish culminated in an esthete's analogy.

♀

The antipodes of love

"Mae West annihilated two of the most famous types in all literature, the seductress . . . whose love changes men into beasts . . . and . . . the opposite . . . the delicate lady shrinking from the advances of brutal men."

CRITICS of culture were by no means the chief participants in this hundred years' war between two contradictory opinions of the proper sphere, exact duty, and precise nature of American women. Literature itself, animated by a similar debate, came eventually to conceive even more daring and convincing modes of resolution. We are accustomed to think, however, that genteel writers subscribed to a single order of belief, a common code which decreed that human character and social institutions were clearly and easily defined, that the success of both was assured if society aimed high and provided steady discipline, firm punishment. Romantic love was blessed because it employed man's "higher" faculties — altruism, piety — and the other was depraved because it evoked certain "lower" traits — greed, lust, irreverence. In life and art, women were placed above men in the ladder of love; their duty was to teach the lesson of self-denial. Except for certain notable works, therefore, American writing of the period lacks tension, drama, conviction. Because it had very little understanding of the whole complex matter of love, genteel fiction was deprived of real men and women, and became little more than a proper form of entertainment — a watered wine to enliven long evenings in the dispirited lives of thin ladies. This situation, in part, caused Hawthorne and Howells to fret, Mrs. Wharton and Henry James to live abroad, others to complain that American culture was in the grip of an iron madonna.

This is not, however, an adequate image of this segment of the American past. The dehumanization of American art is merely one —

by no means the most formidable — effect of genteel morals. Commitment to the romantic ideal was only the first and least intelligent decision, idolatry of angelic women simply one mode of genteel fiction. Indeed, a leading motive of polite letters was to demonstrate that sexual desire could animate even the best men and women, to establish a new vision of love, a new harmony in the relations between the sexes. Shortly before the Civil War, people began to wonder whether the genteel code had not suppressed precisely that vigor, that sense of human integrity — that élan — on which Americans prided themselves and for which the New World was a most compelling symbol. These speculations occur first in the popular fiction of the time. Then, after the War, serious literature too, more and more openly, reasserted half-forgotten values. Suiting its new attitudes to the mood of the day, it stressed the dignity of the individual, his right to fulfill himself, his right, indeed, to *be* himself — whether in politics, business, war, or love.

In order to recognize the effects of this reappraisal, we must return for a moment to the time when the genteel code was first formulated. Although its discipline was perhaps most severe at mid-century, the code itself had resulted from a counterattack on the Age of Reason. Between 1790 and 1830 social, political, and theological liberalism were stridently opposed: Fisher Ames and John Adams chose the principle of property as the soundest substructure for economics and government. William Cobbett and Joseph Dennie composed broadsides against Paine and Godwin, against advanced ideas in theology and morals. And this reaction was exaggerated by a kind of horror at the revolution in France, which Americans understood was modeled on their own. France seemed to be careening Time's chariot in an effort to outrace the future. Although the generation that came to power in 1800 elected Jefferson as its president, nevertheless it opposed many of the positions which that "infidel" spoke for. Manufacture gained prestige over agriculture, revivalism over deism, religionism over natural science. And a nation that faced wars of attrition with the Indians and with England, that could scarcely define its geographical frontier, was impelled to establish a very specific frontier in morals. Thus, as is well known, it adapted to its special purpose the Scottish philosophy of common sense.

No less commonsensical, indeed no less characteristically native, was another kind of adaptation which till now criticism has overlooked. Almost to a man, historians of our letters agree that the forms, the ideas, the manners, and the morals which shape the genteel tradition were taken over from Richardson and Sterne, from the sentimental English novel and the novel of sensibility. Only one of their number makes any distinction to speak of—"The ideal woman of the mid-century still resembled her ancestors, Pamela and Clarissa . . . but she was much changed"—though even he tends to blur crucial distinctions.[1] The customary portrait of the genteel heroine shows us a creature "released from the defunct Gothic romance and the moribund historical romance . . . drafted into the service of the domestic novel, given a course of intensive religious training, taught maneuvers of the heart by Jane Eyre, and assigned to heavy emotional duty on the domestic front."[2]

This statement—and the attitude it reports—is accurate only as it describes the genre and its origins, only in its sense of the surfaces of things. The writers who organized the canon of gentility did indeed borrow some elements of form from the English masters—even from Fanny Burney—but they molded these according to shapes ordered by the American experience itself. Only at the outset, in the late eighteenth century and very early in the nineteenth century, was the novel of sensibility taken over, almost unchanged, into our fiction. W. H. Brown's *The Power of Sympathy* and Hannah Foster's *The Coquette* were novels that dealt in rape, seduction, and suicide in order to teach young American women an Old World lesson. They were shown how to withstand any assault on their virtue, however subtly conceived or guilefully made, and thereby were taught how to avoid loss of reputation.

But fiction of this sort, sheer imitation of the English sentimental novel, flourished for a very short time. Its center of attention shifted most sharply in the period following the revolution in France which, as I have remarked, spread a sudden and intense alarm among certain important conservative leaders. Men such as Timothy Dwight, imagining that French ideas encouraged debauchery, described how a triumph of infidelity and immorality would overrun America if French doctrine were adopted here. Those who are taught by the accursed French illuminati, he said, learned that "chastity and natural affection" are mere "groundless prejudices." He warned that these ideas must be expelled from America, else men would see their "wives and daughters the victims of legal prostitution; soberly dishonoured; speciously polluted; the outcasts of delicacy and virtue; and the loathing of God and man." [3] The rhetoric was of the usual kind and the argument itself seemed credible because French visitors had been, on occasion, indiscreet. Talleyrand, for example, had exhibited his mulatto mistress in Philadelphia. Occasions of this sort encouraged American clergymen to equate deism and rationalism with profligacy and voluptuousness.

Writers enlisted on the side of the angels and turned out sentimental romances designed to serve as antidotes to the French poison. It was this job which Cooper virtually reserved for himself, and by the time he achieved his best work women had lost moist flesh, gained dry salvation. Divested of gross appetites and invested by God with the supreme resources of the spirit, Cooper's heroines are profoundly dedicated to the Church. Men may be noble but they have very little respect for the Church itself or for traditional pieties. This idea of a woman's role — to lead men, corroded by the French or the flesh, back to the true God — informs Cooper's *Wing and Wing* where, in one of its final scenes, Cooper organized in a single, coherent event that cluster of ideas which underlay the New Conservatism of his day. Raoul, a man of science, is dying; the heroine, Ghita, a girl of ineffable gentleness and holiness, hovers:

> "Dost thou know, Ghita . . . that the learned of France tell us that yonder night stars are worlds . . . to which the earth appears but as a star itself?"
>
> "And what is this, Raoul, to the power and majesty of Him who created the universe?"

Man may be seduced by his own intellect, Cooper says, but Woman instinctively knows the Truth: Raoul believes that man's mind is surely his "highest quality; that which makes him Lord of the earth." Ghita replies that his mind is a mere fragment of "the spirit of God himself." An hour passes, Raoul moves closer to death and Ghita prays for his salvation. Suddenly, his "soul was agitated by novel sensations" and he realizes that "chance never made a world" for "some all-powerful hand must have created it." This is Ghita's and God's victory—Raoul is saved. "For months Ghita had not known an instant as happy as that. It appeared as if the mind of Raoul were about to extricate itself from the shallow philosophy so much in fashion."[4]

Almost from the first, therefore, the genteel ethic was designed to cage the evil that surges in men's souls, an evil which liberal theology and scientific inquiry had appeared to release. The clergy and most early novelists hoped to frighten society back to church, but they fought for a lost cause. Americans preferred to remain away and to compose a new secular dogma which would make passion unobtrusive, orthodox, orderly: they created the idea of the Secular Manly. Practical men who were occupied with the problems of settling and operating a new society—with Congress, Indians, canals—later simplified the whole matter by adopting an easy convention: good women embodied a living victory of the spirit over the flesh. Conviction of this sort did not require attendance at church; America itself became a cathedral. Womanliness came to mean sexlessness and in the 1840's and later, fiction relied on this conviction whenever it presented an ideal woman.[5] "Her manners and looks were so . . . spiritual . . . and her soul seemed to be shining through and glorifying her . . . frail body." Manliness came to imply a taste for souls, not bodies. "I like a woman who comes and lays her soft, pure palm in mine, knowing that I am a man . . . [who prizes] the passing angel, and will entertain it honorably and well."[6] And marriage was conceived as a state very much like Swedenborg's vision of life after death, where "men who gravitate toward goodness are taken in charge of a good angel and divinely educated up to higher and higher planes of spiritual beauty."[7] The chief difference between this and earlier forms of

Platonism is that marriage itself provides the occasion for eternal beatitude.

Before mid-century, then, gentility developed a literature of its own. A domesticated American version of English writing in the age of sensibility, it conceived its own idiom, its own code, and its own characteristic heroine. Like English fiction, it chose those women who possessed a certain wizardry of the spirit; American girls, however, put their genius to work on specifically national problems. Of course they continued to share certain traits with sentimental English heroines. Both had God's ear: their prayers were not expressions of devotion but consultations with a Colleague. And when they prayed they were pretty certain of a reply. Customarily God informs them that they are doing very well indeed and must continue to speak for Him. Man is "born of flesh" and is "heir to its temptations," God reminds one heroine, but "one free ardent sigh," borne upon her "wings to Calvary's height, can have the potency to banish . . . *all* the contending powers of ill." [8] The plot in which an American girl appeared most often showed her as the only child of a poor widow, "fearing nothing, doubting nothing, achieving much good and inclined to patient endurance . . . of human weakness." [9] She makes manly men — who don't have time to attend church — "the better for the companionship of innocent maidenhood, and stronger to wrestle with temptations." [10]

But unlike English heroines, these women were not simply pious ladies of exquisite sensibility. On the contrary, the genteel heroine was a woman of destiny. Her grave purpose was not merely to refine and spiritualize men and ennoble civilization, as too often our historians claim.[11] Rather, her aim was to inspire her man and point him, spirit braced, down the high road traveled by all true Americans who undertake to achieve for their nation its manifest destiny.[12] In the back of her mind, religious orthodoxy was fused with messianic patriotism. It was this unique combination of qualities that underlay her effect. Not only does it distinguish genteel heroines from their predecessors, but also it identifies the main reason why women were so highly regarded in the new society.

Even in dime novels, it provides an American woman with a special luster, as we see in an early story about the American revolution when the heroine responds to an Englishman's proposal of marriage. "Oh, Lieutenant Goodheart . . . my love, which you value far too highly, is reserved for my country . . . and its sons." The American hero, standing by, immediately offers himself and asks if she is already affianced. "'I spoke but in general terms,' said Isabelle, her lustrous eyes cast down upon the floor, 'when I referred to the sons of my country. My heart is individually free.'"[13] And the young American, girding his genteel loins, ready to defeat the English single-handed, answers: "That admission gives a vigor to my life . . . and an impulsiveness to hope." Once genteel letters introduced this opinion of womanly purpose into its canon of crucial ideas, our writing became an amalgam of a very special sort, an adaptation not an imitation of earlier modes and genres.

This heroine flourished during the first sixty years of the century and thereafter she faded. If we disregard for a moment the specific forces in America that established this ideal, we recognize an abiding human concern. Its history expresses itself in two entirely different kinds of women—Penelope and Circe, Caesar's wife and Cleopatra, Beatrice and Vittoria Colonna, Cordelia and Goneril—the lily maid and the beautiful, merciless woman of passion. This antithesis identifies one of the marks of western civilization—the clash between sexual denial and assertion, fear and joy, good and evil. We recall how fascinating to the nineteenth-century European mind were enchantresses, women whose charm was irresistible though fatal. In England they became famous when the Gothic mood was popular—first Keats exploited their effect, then Coleridge, Swinburne, and Rossetti; in France they appear in the work of Sade, Stendhal, and Rimbaud. Mario Praz attributes their celebrity to a persistent human perverse joy in the identity of beauty and death. His conception fits American experience, however, in only a minor way, for Americans modified both extreme positions.

In the most famous tale of its day, Oliver Wendell Holmes's *Elsie Venner*, the girl is magnificently malign only until the final moment, and then she recants. A similar idea is developed in a story in which the hero meets a girl who dresses in a leopard skin and radiates "hot sunlight from under the full, heavy lids." It is unusual to find in our writing a full-blown enchantress in the European manner, "perfect as a . . . lotus flower, a still, gorgeous, tropical sunset." And though the hero admires her he knows he is playing with fire—"You are so still! You only look at me, Leonie, your eyes are killing me—a slow, delicious . . ." Suddenly the whole affair goes up in smoke—a burning candle accidentally sets fire to her clothes; the hero saves her but burns his hand. The writer resorted to that homily with which women have been warned against total commitment in love even in the present day—once initiated forever enslaved. "You saved my life . . . it belongs to you now . . . Oh . . . I love you." But our hero is not a European; he is not equipped to accept so gross an attachment and he retreats, attempting "to collect his scattered sense."[14] He turns instead to a warm-hearted Western girl, for what he wants is not a woman of boundless passion but a simpler person. He rejects, too, the woman of boundless virtue for by the time of the Civil War a woman of this kind was no longer taken very seriously. Often she is either seduced or jilted and she dies bereft of her senses or deprived of her traditional niche in society. After 1860 Americans of even the straitest gentility preferred girls with spunk.

European gorgons kill their men but American gorgons, like American angels after mid-century, are unfulfilled. They reform and die or are deserted by their lovers. And when Cooper's opinions and style lost their influence; when the colonial republic began to take the form of an expanding democracy—then a new sensibility appeared to which neither side of the old conflict was completely persuasive. The Yankee trader and the frontiersman, practical men, would playfully quail before a good woman's sharp eye and try hard to behave well. In private they would tell stories about their last escapades. And they were not inclined to worry that bad women would reduce them to gibbering idiots.

By mid-century, too, new attitudes toward marriage helped to simplify this problem, and these attitudes stemmed, in turn, from a new awareness of feminine talents. It was difficult to idolize the American woman who a moment earlier could have killed an Indian. The behavior of large numbers of American women differed profoundly from that usual elsewhere, and this fact helped to create a new conception of marriage. In Europe you preferred your mistress to the wife whom it was a social and filial duty to marry. But in America your wife was your mistress whom it was both wrong and right to desire and whose duty was to discourage desire but to submit. There sexual initiation was earlier, more complicated and ritualistic; here it was perhaps less exciting but it carried a less formidable onus. In Europe passion possessed a kind of splendor but its dangers filled the imagination. In America it was derogated and prized but its sole legitimate place was in marriage. The condition of domesticity was supposed to save a man from the fires of hell and provide him with the hope of heaven because it placed him in the care of a good woman whose job was to assuage but dampen his ardor. The true American man was supposed to "respect his wife nonetheless while he loves her, and find in marriage the true sphere and controlling law of his passional emotions."[15]

The main effort of genteel fiction, therefore, was not to parade a group of idealized or vicious women but somehow to reconcile the two. This was not a simple problem, because writers depended upon the support of a host of novel-reading women—the only sizable audience for literature. And these women, said a particularly acute observer of the effects of "sentimentalism" on society, "cannot bear to look on guilt and vice as they are in themselves." Men try to distract them by devising terms such as "passional attraction" and "elective affinity." "Call it by its true name, lust." During the latter part of the century and almost until the World War, American writers tried to find a form which presented the shameful but insistent claims of "lust" but did not strip "idealism from passion."[16]

When we try to decide when this impulse first was formulated in literature, we discover that Poe's method, in 1838 when he wrote "Ligeia," was to become a kind of norm. He imagined two women, one voluptuous and the other fleshless, vacillated between the two, and finally decided for a combination of the best qualities of each. The vocabulary is, of course, peculiarly his but his impulse is common. Ligeia has "the radiance of an opium dream" and though she is "most violently a prey to the tumultuous vultures" of passion, she has an "ethereal nature." This mixture of saintliness and sex is dramatized by the plot itself: Ligeia dies and the narrator marries Rowena, "fair-haired and blue-eyed," demure, genteel, dull. But she dies too, and Poe chose the scene where the hero sits in the death watch as the best place to clarify his idea. He sees his wife's figure rise from the pallet and suddenly, instead of Rowena's golden locks, he discovers "huge masses of long and dishevelled hair . . . blacker than the raven wings of midnight"; and he stares into the "black and the wild eyes . . . of the Lady Ligeia." In Poe's fantasy the two women blend because neither is perfect: Ligeia though incomparable is a tigress and Rowena though sweet is a lamb. The ideal woman is somehow awesome but also benign, both pure and passionate.[17] She seemed, as Melville was to say in *Mardi*, "Hautia and Yillah connected."

To establish this ideal, to phrase it in various pairs of epithets—such as Emerson's in the poem, "Days": these he called the daughters of time and saw moving in an endless file, bringing both "diadems and fagots"—this was the main effort of literature. For only American women, European travelers were accustomed to say, were at once demure and accessible; they alone combined "the charm of eternal womanliness with the aroma of a progressive century."[18] And after Poe, even the least talented writers realized that American audiences were responsive to a limited amount of erotic undertone. In the fifties and during the sixties and seventies we read stories in which heroines have a kind of gamy virtue. Poor girls wear vines in their hair and are pursued by rich men; prim girls skate on thin ice and nearly drown. These women are vivid and sprightly rather than sallow and flat. Although it is still easier for a gentleman to worship the memory of an angel than to love a girl, he resents the code that enforces this principle. Love is still a threat but what is unique is the way these people are forced to confront sex.

Instead of stories about benign women who are tortured by forces that control them, we read about girls who are destroyed because they cannot adapt themselves to the system. "I thought her at first," a man says about his dead wife, "too far above human nature to be loved by a man, and at length I found myself worshipping her . . . I did reverence to her." His troubles begin when one day, shortly before their marriage, he inquires if she had ever loved anyone else. She admits that she had had an earlier lover who "kissed her often — on the cheek, and forehead and lips — and she had kissed him perhaps as often." He is distressed by this discovery but "her eyes looked down any distrust — those splendid eyes." This girl is obviously respectable but she is also competent in love. Once they are married, the man wonders if she is faithful — he has no adequate reason to doubt her but he realizes that his wife is a woman of vigor. One day he sees her in another man's carriage; he whips his horse and pursues; the carriage is wrecked and the woman, though uninjured, is somehow unhinged. "In her ravings she seemed to be struggling with some terrible enemy, fighting constantly with a fiend." To the American audience these ravings were familiar — they were the obvious consequence of sin. Actually, this woman was innocent and the reason for the appearance of the "fiend" is the writer's wish to identify his heroine's sexual quality and protest her punishment. "I dare not say that she was an angel, or a fit companion for them — but — look at that portrait and tell me, did God make that — all that — for dust or woe?"[19] Can a woman be so pure as society insists, is sex so degrading as men are led to believe?

This question echoed in the minds of insulated gentlemen and whaleboned ladies particularly during the Civil War and afterwards. Between 1860 and 1880, society learned the lesson of violence: indeed the War was in effect a prelude to the battle for power, position, wealth to which at this time the whole culture was committed. And a homely, naive, genteel opinion of human nature and the destiny of this nation could scarcely discipline private soldiers in war or captains of industry in peace. New answers to this pressing question about the place and meaning of sex, therefore, had to be composed for a society in which human energy and vitality suddenly were given high value.[20]

Perhaps it was an image of blood on the battlefield that first established a startled sense of the body's ways and quality, respect for its quickness, horror at its waste in prudery or war. In any event an early sign of this new admiration of vital men and women occurs in fiction which chose as its subject certain recurrent moral problems caused by the War. This literature portrayed a conflict in the heroine's soul where the lure of desire contends with the staid principles of virtue to which she has been bred. Actual war is transposed—the stories say nothing about the Civil War because, of course, writers knew almost nothing about it—into a battle between hot Southern sinners and cold Northern saints. A Southern man is by definition peccant and his lure is sweet but terrible; a Southern woman—she is called Alabama Russell or something similar—has "a dangerous fiend peering out of her shining hazel eyes." Defeat of the South was therefore a victory of the forces of modesty and honor over the forces of indulgence and lust; chastity over carnality, good over evil. "Cold winters and short summers," says a writer on New England women, have "brought to perfection the rarest, purest 'woman' . . . in all the world." "Diana's crescent, pure and pale, rises over that fortunate land which surrounds" Plymouth Rock. "Puritan morality, Puritan prejudice, Puritan purity"—the rhetoric is ambitious but tortured—have created in Northern women "a sort of passion for chastity." A Southern woman, he decided, is nevertheless "delicious."[21]

In fiction these ideas form a kind of allegory in which the chaste Northern girl personifies virtue and the fiery Southern man personifies vice.

> "Yes . . . you loved me . . . with a sober saintly affection; not with the irrepressible fervor that fires the Southern heart."
>
> "My love would have sacrificed all just things for you; yours would not give up a depraved appetite for me," I replied. He held my flower in his hand . . .[22]

And although the North was on the side of the angels, somehow its position lacked not only charm but also conviction. In the most common of many similar plots, a Southerner is stranded in the North at the beginning of the War. He loves a native girl and urges her to return with him despite the conflict in their loyalties. She refuses. He goes alone, is wounded in battle, taken prisoner, hospitalized in the place where his beloved is a nurse. They see each other for a moment before he dies and he chooses this moment to tell her that she was sacredly right, he devilishly wrong. The plot, therefore, expresses public morals. But it is not the plot that reports his effect upon the girl, her responsiveness to the energy that impels his love. These are demonstrated by images which were cliché even by 1870. She wears "some sort of scarlet vine running like fire through her hair"; the man has "a dark, deep face, that wore its dusky beauty like a mask." He struggles to keep "cool . . . control . . . of the fire that leapt to the eyes"—the lush Southerner become a Byronic hero. As they dance she imagines that she "scents" the odor of magnolia groves, that they share a common "magnetism." He crushes her "tress of golden hair" with "vehement pressure against . . . bearded lips"—she thrills and he glows: this hair could "kindle a less ardent imagination . . . than this young Carolinian's." Despite hair, magnetism, and the rest, the people always separate and always when they meet again the man says in final unction, "Do not weep . . . You were right." [23]

A war over slavery, therefore, provided writers of American subliterature with a useful method for representing a conflict which had nothing to do with the War itself. The plot was popular through the seventies, and in the next decade it entered the main line of our literature in Henry James's *The Bostonians*. This novel is supposedly about feminism, but James's main purpose was to trace effects of a confused system of morals upon the relations between men and women in America: "feminism" is a euphemism for sex. James chose a group of people in whom the essence of love had become distorted or vulgarized: Olive Chancellor, "a spinster as Shelley was a lyric poet"; her sister, Mrs. Luna, literally delicious but dull: "her hair was in clusters of curls, like bunches of grapes; her tight bodice seemed to crack with her vivacity . . . She was attractive and impertinent, especially the latter." By impertinent James meant mindless and unrestrained rather than irreverent; she is an uninteresting woman in whom love is a pose and a posture. Between these extreme people James placed Verena Tarrant, who inherits her vigor from her father, a charter member of the free-love Cayuga Community. Thus she inherits from him a special talent for love — which James symbolized in her gift of inspirational speech — but she inherits, too, a radical misunderstanding of its meaning. Despite her gift, her beauty — her red hair seemed "to glow with the brightness of her nature" — her sensibility, she allows herself to be used by feminists and to plead their cause. Olive Chancellor "buys" her from her father and urges her to exhibit herself in behalf of the woman's rights movement.

Into this throng of enthusiasts, free lovers, petticoats, and pedants who are identified as the leading spokesmen in American life, James introduced his hero, Ransom. His job is to claim Verena from that group so that society will be saved from it, and indeed, from itself. "The most salient and peculiar point in our social life," James said in his *Notebooks*, reflecting on the problems that led him to this novel, is the "decline in the sentiment of sex." [24] Ransom's duty is to stop this decline by weaning a lovely, brilliant woman from her folly. Saving Verena from Olive Chancellor, Ransom saves her from neuroticism and impotence. Through marriage she will adapt her gifts to society at large; Ransom persuades her that her force, properly used, will make her "the most charming woman in America" because she will endow "the sentiment of sex" with a new dignity. This in turn will mold anew the life of society.

James required a man of power, therefore, and he decided to go South: he relied on the myth of Southern eroticism to underscore Ransom's effect. Composing this novel in order to propose a sexual revolution, James's imagination sought images that evoked the idea of Southern virility. Ransom's Southern speech, he said, was "pervaded by something sultry and vast, something almost African in its rich basking tone, something that suggested the teeming expanses of the cotton field." In James's view, Ransom is a man who can overcome Northern enervation and sterility: his moral duty is to recover the masculine character in America. The union between Ransom and Verena, between the fabulous, heated, fertile South and the cold, repressed North would reconcile two extreme positions in American morals. Verena, fulfilled in marriage, would assert her influence over a wide arid ground: it "will irrigate, it will fertilize . . . will become really social."[25]

James's novel displeased his audience because it separated passion from idealism: the stately middle classes continued to prefer reserve to candor and to admire fiction that shaded its truths with cant. James, choosing a Southern hero, realized that his audience would recognize the man's erotic power; simultaneously, choosing a man of will and energy, a former soldier, a gentleman of law out to recover his estate, he knew that it would respect Ransom on still another ground—as a man of action. But he did not foresee that his audience would reject Ransom's diagnosis of the American malady. For society, willing to respond to a kind of euphemized virility, was not yet able to admire men who exercised this quality in the matter of love itself. Like James, it respected men of passion; unlike James, it expected these men to adore money and to order their lives according to the gospel of wealth.

Expansion in business and politics, therefore, was accompanied by a certain dilation in morals. Men were no longer forced to worship women.[26] Everyone realized that what distinguished the man of action was not his virtue but his vigor, his independence. He was peremptory and cocksure rather than docile and subdued, gentlemanly. A generation earlier, men who were self-willed, passionate, who rejected the common morality, had only one recourse. They could head West. After the War, however, society gave the highest prestige to those rugged individualists who cornered the markets or created great corporations or, in the fashion of W. L. Newberry of Chicago, consumed large blocks of cheap real estate that were soon to have enormous value. "Almost any clever young man," says a girl in Henry B. Fuller's story, "New Wine," should be able "to roll up a few hundred thousand dollars within a few years"—"no others, of course, count." The pursuit of wealth, conceived as the most telling evidence of human uniqueness, importance, individuality, was in effect the most convincing sign of malehood. This idea was reinforced by the growing conviction that the genteel ideal may have assured virtue but, dissipating desire, it also suffocated zeal — the urge to build, to transform the wilderness, to create.

The ideal of rugged manliness did not, perhaps, actually create new attitudes toward women but it did breed new expectations, a new sensibility. Vigorous men required lively women, and girls who had grown up during the holocaust were indeed less demure. Instead of imitating the fashion plates in *Godey's*, for example, many modeled themselves according to the fashion set by Princess Eugenie in France.[27] A furtive and shamed sense of the structure of the human body was replaced by the impulse to display, to flatter its shape, to stress its invitation. Men reacted by mocking women who tried too hard, who used "all sorts of artificial substitutes — her bosom heaves with sighs of cotton and her whole figure swells with an emotion of starch and crinoline." And they described their ideal — which *Harper's* printed in 1868, though an opinion of this sort would have been unthinkable ten years earlier: "Buffon says that 'a woman's breasts to be well-placed should be separated by a space equal to that between the nipple and the centre of the hollows on the collar bone. They should be, moreover, small, solid, gently rounded and not too firmly attached.' "[28]

The new sensibility helped to mold fiction which does not quite reject the old code but instead tries to modify and supplement. Gentlemen who lament the death of angelic ladies are replaced by rich brisk young men who admit that they admire women "of a sensual kind" and therefore prefer a "well-developed form to the finest countenance." If a girl is too virtuous, inflexible, if she believes that the manners of the day are sinful, usually she dies a martyr in the cause of gentility. For the leading heroines of the day are more pliant, their virtue more viable. They possess a form of purity that reminds us of Cooper's ideal, alongside a kind of marginal innocence that foreshadows the leading quality of women in fiction since the First World War. No longer is she a dewdrop. She is a "dahlia . . . eyes black . . . heavy black hair, a brilliant color, and a full, buxom figure."[29] In protest against "two hundred years of strait lacing," we learn, the "little Puritans" buried Diana's crescent and "changed roles with the witches."[30] And they were more charming than ever. For though they were good enough to be respectable they were suggestive enough to be desirable: they combined a "positively magnetic effect" with "affectations of prudery."[31]

But society was unprepared for a revolution. It was not yet ready to reconcile matter and spirit, flesh and soul, to commit itself to an entirely new principle, a symbiosis of love. As a result it preferred Howells to James. For it was Howells who conserved the protest against strait lacing by refining and domesticating but never defining its appeal. His usual method was to insist that his heroine was an angel, that she never had an idea that she could not tell her maiden aunt. Then he placed her in a situation that contradicted this opinion and compromised the girl. What results is a *jeune fille* without dewdrops, Howells's subtle variant of the theme of mixed magnetism and prudery. He never admits that his heroine can know vulgar passion but he replaces the dew with laudanum and urges us to notice the shadows beneath the eyes. His subtlety actually outstripped the intelligence of his audience which, confused, was undecided about his motives. "All through the early eighties," his disciple, Hamlin Garland, remarked, "Boston was divided into two parts — those who liked Howells and those who fought him, and the most fiercely debated question . . . was whether his heroines were true to life, or whether they were caricatures." Howells was actually condemned for his "injustice to the fair sex."[32]

He sowed this confusion because he believed that sex was a disparagement of virtue. And his stories almost invariably concern girls who are guiltless but condemned. His motive was not Kafka's — he did not transmute the woman's situation into a statement on the human condition. Instead he represented in one heroine those ideas about virtue and vice which long had shaped society's opinion of love and which Poe and others had required two people to express. Love inexorably involves desire and this fact taints even the most angelic woman. Her evil may be projected to her family: in

The Son of Royal Langbrith, the girl resembles her father who eats opium and is insane; in *An Imperative Duty,* the American Girl discovers that her grandmother was a Negro. Or it may be located in a compromising event: Lydia Blood in *The Lady of the Aroostook,* for example, crosses the Atlantic on a ship where she is the only lady among three gentlemen and the crew. Even her Europeanized aunt is shocked by the impropriety but she disdains the aunt's criticism: "From the time the ship sailed until I reached this wicked place, there wasn't a word said or a look looked that made me think that I wasn't just as right and safe as if I had been in my own room at home." This is unconvincing, however, because she had allowed a drunken rake to make love to her. He had been sent by his family on a salubrious sea journey and she had decided to help in his reform. Her innocence is nevertheless tarnished, as it is when an Italian mistakes her for a loose woman because she travels alone. Howells damned that obscene European cast of mind which misconceives independence for sensuality but neither his disclaimer nor hers is persuasive. The divine Lydia is simply not entirely respectable and everyone agrees, finally, that the hero is right to take her to California where she is anonymous. Recalling the anguish of the Lapham sisters, Marcia Gaylord's passionate jealousy, we try to find a serene or untainted woman and we discover only one, Margaret Vance of *A Hazard of New Fortunes.* And her destiny is to be a nun.

The leading heroine of genteel fiction, then, is neither an angel nor a devil but somehow she joins the benignity of the first with the piquancy of the second. It was this image of American women, of course, that held the European imagination. What she symbolized, Paul Bourget explained, was "neither sensuality nor tenderness" but a combination of the two. American society came to accept the world's opinion of its achievement. Although it was accustomed to believe that ardor indicated radical depravity of the soul, it tried to discount the fact that ardent men and women were attractive, lively people. To represent this conflict, writers decided on a common group of images and seized occasions, such as the Civil War, provided by history. For they realized that American civilization would not flourish until it encouraged larger freedom in the individual conscience, until it recognized the joy and honor of love. It was Howells, finally, who organized society's decisions and indecisions: his double-talk displayed and masked America's double vision. Forcing his substantial talent to remain within the limits of the genteel code, he exploited the conscience of his generation in order to titillate it with his discoveries. As a result, he established this heroine's place in the American imagination and her fame in our literature. Gibson's portraits adorned the apartments and Howells's heroines peopled the fantasies of the men at Harvard, for these girls seemed best to represent a middle ground between the antipodes of love.

They were competing, however, with a very formidable person, the girl of the golden West. And it was this image not Howells's which seemed far more convincing: Western women had, after all, the advantage of geography — of a tradition in which the ideas of health, freedom, and vitality reinforced the appeal of the wilderness and of love.

The lily and the prairie flower

"Margaret Truman happens to be just a Midwestern Girl used to moving around [who] . . . could take in her stride a Washington society in which her old farming friends and Kansas City boys juggle drinks with ambassadors and lawyers. If she had been what they call a well-brought-up Eastern girl, I think she would have been more likely to blush and stumble at Buckingham Palace and Versailles."

IN AN EFFORT to establish national unity by settling the wilderness, Easterners left ravaged forests for the big fir on Puget Sound; poor farms for plush lands; the small shops in which fishermen and hired hands were doomed to work in the long off-season for loaded rivers and massed prairies. And these migrants were led by an image of Western fertility which, historically, had animated the European imagination in the seventeenth and eighteenth centuries: America was a new Eden. But they were impelled, too, to establish national coherence in a continent whose resources and structure were known only in a most general way. Geographical definition was somehow antecedent to political and economic harmony. And national self-definition, the prime aim of society at large, was inseparable from economics, politics, and geography. During the settlement of the West, therefore, a society that tended to think in antitheses and to yearn for unity discovered a new symbolism. In literature, the East was substituted for the North and the West replaced the South.

This was a valid exchange because the most striking fact about the movement is that it drew an enormous number of Yankees. In 1787, the first covered wagon left Ipswich Hamlet, Massachusetts; during the decade 1850–1860, more than half a million New Englanders undertook the long journey. By 1870 the census showed that in California, for example, nearly four fifths of the residents had come from the Northeast.[1] And when we regard the consciously regional literature of New England, we realize that this search for a land of the heart's desire involved a protest not only against frigid soil but also against arid morality. What these people wished to escape is implicit in the fiction of Harriet Beecher Stowe or Sarah Orne Jewett or Mary E. W. Freeman but it is explicit indeed in the advice given to Sophia Peabody—Hawthorne's wife-to-be. After years of despair, in 1833 Sophia took a sea voyage. Feeling better, she joyfully wrote her news to her mother who replied, "Perhaps no one better than myself can appreciate the benefit past years of pain have been to you. They have formed for you a character at once lovely and elevated, correcting, subduing, eradicating self-sufficiency, pride, obstinacy . . . And now that your Father and mine sees fit to give you the enjoyment of tolerable health, you will devote all the energies of your enthusiastic and glowing mind to His Service and Glory."[2] This grandiose and inhumane discipline produced pallid people who suffered and endured, or rebellious men and women who fled to the Garden of the World. The women who endured their suffering appear in fiction a generation later: their chief quality is their desire to love and to live but they are incapable of committing themselves either to a man or to life itself. This whole habit of mind is epitomized in a story by Mrs. Freeman which employed a familiar symbolism. The lover asked the heroine for one of the lilies in her basket. "I wanted to give him one of those flowers more than anything else in the world! I . . . had my fingers on the stem of the finest lily there . . . I stood still gazing at him . . . As I gazed, his face changed more and more . . . till finally—I cannot explain it—it looked at once beautiful and repulsive. I wanted at once to give him the lily and would have died rather than give it to him, and I turned and fled."[3] Conceiving marriage to embody the repulsive anguish and beautiful joy of desire, Northern women of the nicest sensibilities chose spinsterhood.

New England, filled with stillborn or dying generations, was clearly no place for the young. And those girls who did not think that "celibacy [is] the higher condition" set off for the West.[4] As early as 1837 "a wagonload of girls for the Western market" passed through Northampton, Massachusetts.[5] In 1866 Mercer organized his second shipload of young women gathered from Maine, Massachusetts, New York, New Jersey, and Maryland. They were drawn by an image of domesticity with a healthy Adam which old myths had created and a new literature proclaimed, by the hope that life in the West would be freer and riper than life elsewhere. For the belief that life at the frontier encouraged a new vigor in the relations between men and women had appeared early in the literature of the West. Caroline Kirkland's *A New Home—Who'll Follow?* claimed that the area was peopled by free men and blithe women; Alice Cary wrote stories in which a typical Westerner was an "independent yeoman" of "simple rusticity and healthful habits." And in the fifties and sixties this image was reproduced in the wild Western hero whose freedom from Eastern forms of moral bigotry, Charles Webber wrote, was based in his freedom from "all shackles upon the physical life." Such men depend upon "the instincts of their own souls and hearts for what is just and true. To them all that is true, fitting, and natural in a passion, is proper and legitimate."[6] Actually, the situation in the heartland was quite different from the image presented by popular fiction. What fiction defined was not the fact of life in the West but what Easterners hoped to find there. This sense of the wilderness provided Melville with the image of a quiet colt in Vermont who catches the scent of "the savage musk" of buffalo in Oregon and is frenzied. It helped to shape the motives of quiet girls in Vermont, too. And by 1893 when F. J. Turner made his famous speech to the American Historical Association—he announced that the West encouraged man to "grow to the full measure of his own capacity"—this hope had the full sanction of society.

The fantasy of wild Western sexual vitality was indeed a compelling one; it occurs in both popular fiction and serious literature and often concerned the same kind of person. By 1880, Henry Nash Smith has reported, the "drastic weakening of the long prevalent taboos against sexual passion in women" was dramatized by heroines like Hurricane Nell and Calamity Jane, who lighted cigars while riding at full speed, drank whiskey, shot guns, swore like men.[7] That is to say, popular fiction chose women who were as "bad" as men — like the Western hero, they had unusual equipment for love. We know, of course, that this is not the first sign of a weakening of taboos against passion, that Eastern fiction after the Civil War was especially drawn to "magnetic" women. But tales about Hurricane Nell provide a less sophisticated and more dramatic statement of these ideas. Before long, she was tamed and tidied and introduced into Eastern Society where she retained the sexual effect but lost the habits of the Amazon. Provided with skirts instead of buckskin pants, a cart rather than a saddle, she was removed from the usual arena of wild Western fiction and settled in the cities. There she achieved a lustrousness with which Eastern girls, who combined magnetism and prudery, could hardly compete. For the wild women who entered our main literature were healthy, not depraved; they imbibed from the mountain air its purity and its pungency. Gertrude Atherton's heroines, for example, do not merely wear scarlet vines in their golden tresses. Helena, a California debutante, lives the life of Society with the same spirit that Calamity Jane lived the life of the prairie. She has been "engaged fifteen times; she rides about the country in boys' clothes and sits up all night under the trees in Del Monte talking to a man . . . and once went camping alone with five men." Born in California, she had been reared under its "new, savage traditions" and as a result her face shows incipient "cruelty and sensuality" which she tries to mold according to a new ideal of love.[8]

The myth of the Wild Woman of the West, then, created heroines who do not flinch from their passions. This myth had a variant in the concept of the West as a passage to India — Whitman's view. Since the time of Jefferson, indeed, the Pacific Coast had been conceived as a gateway to the Orient, the land of peacocks, ivory, spice. Frank Norris chose these ideas for *Moran of the Lady Letty*; he transferred the action from the prairie or the mountains not because he had something new to say but because he was more comfortable describing love among pirates than among pioneers. The heroine who introduces the hero to the violence of love is simply a Hurricane Nell of the Pacific. Norris made her foreign by birth and a pirate by trade but gave her no quirk of character that distinguished her from the women of the plains. Like them, she is unhampered by genteel civilization; she is savage — that is, passionate; she wears men's clothes — competent in love. "She drank whiskey after her meals, and when angry . . . swore like a buccaneer. As yet she was . . . unconquered, untamed, glorying in her own independence . . . In her men's clothes she looked tall, vigorous, and unrestrained."

Ross Wilbur, a fashionable and idle Western gentleman with an Eastern education, is shanghaied; he and the captain are the only white men among a group of depraved Chinese. The captain is out for a quick killing in ambergris, for everything he can get, when their ship comes upon another, abandoned but for its dead captain and Moran Sterner, his daughter. It is a prize of salvage. The girl is taken against her will, she and Ross mutiny, set out for San Francisco, have adventures which delay them. This leads to the moment when Ross and Moran literally fight to decide who is master. What Norris tried to say is very simple. American men are made foppish by the ethic of gentility but can, when stirred, be virile and capable lovers of even the most vigorous women. But he included another group of ideas which modify this. First, women of passion exist only outside American culture; second, they must be mastered by force; third, once mastered they are forever subdued; but, fourth, their sensuality disqualifies them from society. "It was not Moran whom he fought," Norris explained, "it was her force . . . he set himself to conquer." Once conquered she is transformed, made gentle and womanly — "You've conquered me and . . . I love you for it." But there is no real place in America for this superb animal and Norris returns her to the sea; "alone upon a derelict ship . . . she went out . . . to the great gray Pacific." He conceived this return as a drama of sex in which the sea "that knew her and loved her . . . shouted and called for her, and thundered in the joy of her as she came to meet him like a bride to meet a bridegroom." [9]

When Norris turned to the question of love on land he was far more subdued. And he chose the view of the West which was far more popular than the myth of its wildness; the West as Garden of the World. Instead of a Brunhild he admired a Ceres—Hilma in *The Octopus*: "White neck . . . swell of the breast . . . maturity of her hips . . . exuberant . . . large white arms, wet with milk, redolent and fragrant with milk" and so on.[10] Although Norris pictured Mother Earth, the leading image of lovely Western girls was the flower. Eastern girls drooped but Western girls were described by what we may call a tropism of sex—they drew from their region a certain benign, sweet energy. Unlike Southern girls—whom they replaced in the hierarchy of attractive women—they were not magnolia-ridden erotics. Their odor was invigorating. Often this idea was combined with a certain snobbery and we meet girls like James's Henrietta Stackpole who has "in her garment" the odor of the "great country stretching away beyond the rivers and across the prairies, blooming and smiling and spreading till it stops at the green Pacific." So well-endowed is she that the effect "almost knocks one down."[11]

Ordinarily, however, snobbery was less marked than an extravagant respect for her verve and its influence upon society. There are countless stories about overtrained Easterners and impoverished Europeans who go West, meet a girl who symbolizes "sweetness and beauty and peace with the world"; "a gentle, hopeful assurance of happiness."[12] Through her, they regain their vigor, their self-respect, and their fortune. In Henry Adams's *Esther*, these ideas are so patent that the novel very nearly misses being fiction at all. Esther is a New York girl of high cultivation and inexorable conscience but Catherine is a "mustang," "the cheeriest and healthiest of girls"; she has the "transparency of a Colorado sunrise," and though she is a "young savage," she is "as natural and sweet as a flower." The somber, hypercivilized painter, Wharton, loves her for her strength; discovering in her eyes a "little look of heaven," he wishes to paint her as Saint Cecilia and to marry her. To her mind, however, "ten thousand head" are prettier than "all the saints and naiads" and she refuses him because she plans "to buy a cattle ranch . . . and run it myself."[13] Adams admired Esther's style but Catherine is a Virgin whose sexual energy was enshrined not in Chartres but in the West.

The legend of Western vitality, therefore, was reproduced in many forms during the years of actual migration westward. For the migration itself helped to provide a new vision of love which, everyone believed, was truly authentic to national conditions. Society believed that men who subdued Indians and leveled forests were somehow magically empowered to discover a form of delight which was proscribed and unhealthy elsewhere. Expectation of riches was integrated with high hopes for a new fertility of love in the Garden: Ceres and Venus. These expectations were embodied in heroines who represent a kind of sentimentalism of sex.

Actually, however, this legend had very little more reality than the legend of absolute Eastern gentility. For when we turn to the literature of the Middle West we discover that its experience does not jibe with the myth. Edward Eggleston, E. W. Howe, even Bret Harte portrayed life in the Garden as a life of desperation whose rhythm was fear, scarcity, struggle. They tried to say precisely how it felt to work the fields or the mines all day and expunge the devil all night — and to say this, unlike Clemens, without humor. People in the East and Far West were surprised to discover anguished, bent plodders where they had envisioned lithe yeomen and vibrant women. But what is most impressive about Middle Western writing is not its denial of the myth. It did indeed shape a new morality upon which society could agree and it did achieve an image of unity based in authentic national experience. Sloughing off all sentimental opinions of its culture, this literature portrayed the process through which a confused but undismayed people reconstructed their morality to suit their situation. Drawing on a respect for freedom, a belief in human perfectibility, an admiration of human vigor, these people tried to establish an order that reproduced the best in the old and incorporated the best in the new.

As the West evoked thoughts of unrestrained freedom, so the East reminded Middle Westerners of noble and ancient traditions. And the woman they admired most is usually one whose manners were, in some respects, Eastern. This placed her in the highest caste because it implied that she had a taste for and custom in gentility, restraint. The usual plot centers on a man's struggles to be worthy of her. He must fight the old battle, as Eggleston says, that "Paul described so dramatically when he represented the Spirit as contending with the flesh. Paul . . . called this . . . the old Adam, and I suppose Darwin would call it the remains of the wild beast. But call it what you will, it is the battle that every well-endowed soul must fight at some point."[14] This is the beast to which Frank Norris's Vandover and McTeague succumb. Norris's terms are secular, however, for he did not invoke the religiosity common in the Bible Belt. In Eggleston's *Roxy*, for example, the heroine has a rigorous Methodism which helps her "to save souls in revivals." Once Roxy marries Bonamy, a backslider, her zeal "centered itself in the all-consuming desire to save" her husband.[15]

A very familiar code was obviously adapted to conditions at the frontier. What the rest of the world conceived as a place where companionable barn-raising and corn-husking in the open air dispelled lust was actually a place where the national dilemma was most poignantly felt. Middle Western society, after all, presented few forms in which the relations between the sexes might be ordered. The device of conspicuous display as a form of sexual assertion was denied people who prided themselves on their democracy. And yet courage and self-assertion were crucial for survival. What remained was the brute conflict itself and this Eggleston attributed to the extremes of behavior common to the area. Wild revels "were followed by wild revivals"—the semiannual bacchanal of the circuit tent—and the "grotesque humor and savage ferocity of abandoned wickedness" were contradicted by "austere piety." As we know, the frontier did not create this situation, but merely set in relief perplexities and indecisions common throughout society.

It solved these perplexities in an extraordinary way. Literature insists that unrestrained sexuality is savage and wicked but it insists, too, that an absolute denial of sex seriously disrupts life. As a result its best women avoid either form of extravagance. We meet no wild plainswomen, savage debutantes, pretty prairie flowers.

And even the angels no longer have their traditional role. The uxorious Easterner is by definition a clod to be raised by Psyche; he himself has little to do with his elevation. The Western angel embodies human nobility in its ripest form but the choice is the man's how he responds. Weak men invite their own ruin and end up in Texas or Virginia City; strong men fight the good fight and are reborn but no mere woman can mold their lives — no respectable man would enter heaven tied to his wife's apron strings.

Indeed, she would have turned him out if he had not recognized his own duty in the matter, for even the purest woman rejected the pedestal and preferred the marriage bed. When Bonamy repents of his wickedness, for example, he tells Roxy that he is not fit to say that he loves her. "God knows I worship you," he incants, "I could get down on my knees to you. I would like to be your slave." This was a familiar posture in the East but Roxy knows that homage is pointless. "I don't want that," she tells him.[16] In *The Story of a Country Town*, Howe distinguished between mindless worship and manly acumen precisely because he hoped to define the most productive form of love. He made Mateel, the daughter of an Eastern clergyman, passive, dutiful, "puny," absurd. Jo, her lover, admires her for all the wrong reasons. "Always and everywhere, when my better part is uppermost, she is in my thoughts, but never when I am contemptible in any way." Their marriage fails because Jo's genteel idolatry renders him an unfit husband; "there is not such a woman in the world" as the one he has created, "no such love as he expects," and his life ends in suicide. Thus a form of idolatry which completely denies sex not only disorders love but also deranges the mind.

The other disordered marriage in the novel fails for the classic reason: Reverend John Westlock rejects his noble wife, elopes with an enchantress, and wrecks himself. He is seduced to the life of lust because he wants to escape the corrosions of the life of virtue. "I thought that if I were married to a flashy, ambitious woman, nothing would be impossible."[17] He fails, of course, because sin is wicked. What is striking, however, is Howe's rejection of both extremes, simplistic denial and total commitment. He proposed a sort of middle way: marry the schoolteacher who comes from the East. She is demure and self-reliant, at once self-effacing in good womanly fashion and self-assertive in accord with the custom of the frontier. That is, idealize but do not idolize a woman of vigor.

Although Middle Western writing was unable to say that human passion was blessed, it refused to admit that earthly love was depraved. It did not believe that man was purified by the wilderness. But somehow, in the area far from dirty cities and bad novels, from the overheated Southland, from the antique malice of evil Europe, passion and health were reconcilable. This decision is represented not only in vigorous angels but mainly in tempestuous women. Unlike Eastern gorgons, these girls do not draw their energy from some mystical demonism. Rather, they have an authentic social character—history, antecedents, class. They are not morbid or mysterious. Their leading qualities are beauty, spontaneous emotion, and excess of sexual energy. A woman of this kind is destructive only until she learns to restrain herself; in the rhetoric of the day, she is bad only until she discovers her soul. She springs from a savage race in which the savagery of the region is exaggerated; as the wilderness is subdued her tribe grows sedate and she herself learns to moderate her passions.

Often the girl and her family have emigrated from the South but unlike the Southern belle in Eastern fiction, she is the child of the North Carolina Tarheel or the Louisiana Redneck. Perhaps she is the daughter of a Kentucky frontiersman and a runaway slave girl, of Mike Fink and his mulatto mistress. Her family, says Eggleston, are the "Hoosiers of the dark regions of Indiana and the Egyptians of Southern Illinois." Her birthright is a profound knowledge of Negro lore; its arcana underpin her special competence in love. Like the Negro she is savage but domesticable, a sensual woman with the rudiments of sensibility.

Bret Harte built his career on the lessons in the meaning of love which these women taught. In *Cressy*, a family of this sort has moved deep into the heartland from "Kaintuck" and, like Clemens' Grangerfords, it carried along its special kind of savage vigor. Cressy's father was a "selfish savage and literally red-handed brawler." And her mother, Harte says, was one of those women who "sent their loved ones to hopeless adventure as a matter of course, or with partisan fury; who had devotedly nursed the wounded . . . or had received back their dead dry-eyed and revengeful." Cressy is "the cub of the untamed beast"; her lovely brown hand is little different from the "velvet paw of a young panther." "She bounded to him, and throwing her arms around his neck" said, "You haven't kissed me yet. What's the matter?" She is one of these uprooted Southern girls, she tells the Eastern schoolteacher-hero, "who haven't a nigger to bless themselves with since the War." [18]

If we disregard Harte's addiction to claptrap we realize that he was a very forceful spokesman for the new morality. Indeed, Harte's *M'liss* is actually "Ligeia" writ large and made authentic to American social experience. The girl is a hoyden who "fought the schoolboys with keen invective and quite as powerful arm"; her "fierce, ungovernable disposition . . . and mad freaks and lawless character, were proverbial." Her foil, Clytie, is an ordinary kind of virtuous pretty girl, "neat, orderly and dull." Like Cressy, M'liss learns to be moderate in order to suit the gentleman whom she loves but beneath this veneer, Harte says, her powerful heart still surges. The famous climax to "The Outcasts of Poker Flat," in the same vein, is merely an alternate method of saying similar things; the virginal Piney and the depraved Duchess die in an embrace so close and so leveling that "You could scarcely have told . . . which was she that had sinned." This was Eggleston's method, too. Roxy was "one of God's angels" and Nancy Kirtley—a "magnificent . . . half-oriental animal . . . a perfect gypsey queen of beauty" whose "perfect physical development undisturbed and uninformed by a soul"—is "the Devil's devil." These two women who stand for two quite alien principles, like Piney and the Duchess, finally resolve their difference in an embrace. And when finally Roxy achieved the gesture which unified Eggleston's total vision of love, she symbolized the yearning of a whole civilization. For it dawned on Roxy, Eggleston says, "that she herself had never before in so full a sense embraced the Christ as when she had taken Nancy unto her bosom." [19] Thus Eggleston spoke for his region's conviction that the woman who denies the "Nancy" in herself is at best two thirds a woman, while the one who is merely passionate must be at least "susceptible to good influence" else she is damned. The final effect of this reconciliation is dramatized when Nancy marries a man of her own class and moves further westward—to join, we might say, Cressy and her savage tribe. She leaves Roxy her bastard son, Bonamy's child, and we realize that the future belongs to those people who recognize and harness precisely that force which these writers traced to the most savage members of their communities.

It is this concept that wins the day. Midwestern literature rejected not only the polarities of good and evil but also opinions offered by the sentimentalists of sex. And they made a convincing case for the dignity of love because they showed where its roots were and insisted that these were healthy and strong though perhaps a little ragged. It was their image of unity that became national, and not Howells's or even James's. And certainly it was not Adams's concept, though the energy which Adams had traced to the twelfth century they located deep in America. Perhaps the most vivid portrayal of their vision occurred a few years later, in 1910, when William Vaughn Moody wrote "The Great Divide." Moody improved on their achievement by simplifying it and forcing it to include virtually all ideas about East and West available in his day. The play presents Ruth Jordan, a girl from New England, alone in a cabin out West. A group of raucous, reveling men break in. She promises to marry one of them, Ghent, if he will save her from a fate worse than death. He is a boor—"he eats bacon with his bowie knife . . . has the conversation of a preoccupied walrus . . . and the endearments of a dancing crab in mating season." But she keeps her word and they marry. Later she cannot rid herself of guilt; their marriage, she feels, is profane because in effect she was raped. While Ghent is busy making a fortune she returns to New England. He follows, presents her family a major share of his wealth, and urges her to return with him. She refuses. She argues that their marriage might have succeeded if he had "only heard my cry to you, to wait, to cleanse yourself and me—by suffering and sacrifice . . . But you wouldn't see the need . . . If you could have said, 'The wages of sin is death' and suffered the anguish of death, and risen again purified." The argument leaves him cold. Pointing to the portraits of her Puritan ancestors, he says "It's these fellows are fooling you! It's they who keep your head set on the wages of sin and all that rubbish. What have we to do with suffering and sacrifice?" Finally, Ruth succeeds in understanding Ghent's view and is converted. He speaks for the deep, true American experience which stresses the beauty of man and the sweetness of love. Through "one of the old volcanic rifts in his surface," Ruth sees the "fire, the molten heart of a continent"—what Shakespeare called the true Promethean fire. Once this conversion occurs she realizes that he has "taken the good of . . . life and grown strong. I have taken the evil and grown weak unto death."[20] And she returns to the West, hoping that Ghent will teach her and their children how to live with joy and without terror or guilt.

In "The Great Divide," a wild Westerner of the kind popular in fiction half a century earlier argues an opinion of love which was embodied in the literature of the heartland. And when a woman whom Hawthorne's mother-in-law would have approved of chooses to learn the rites of love, East and West are joined. A nation which produced such women, Europeans felt, had indeed reconciled past and present, innocence and virility, idealism and downrightness—had fulfilled the elaborate yearning of a whole civilization and, in its women, had fused eros and agape.

♀

Fortune's darlings

"In character Wallis was and still remains, complex and elusive, and from the first I looked upon her as the most independent woman I had ever met. This refreshing trait of American women I was inclined to put down as one of the happier outcomes of the event of 1776."

FROM Portland, Maine, to Portland, Oregon, from Chicago to New Orleans — the distance any young lady could travel without chaperon or fear — society agreed that American women best represented the vigor and intensity of the American spirit.[1] Finally on these shores the most trenchantly human dream, the dream of western civilization, the dream of all the ages, was manifested in a lovely woman who, in her own person, reconciled national manners and morals. And her fame abroad far outweighed her effect at home. After the Civil War, when real American girls arrived in Europe, they raised a storm. Feminists and earls fussed over them: "American girls . . . are fast developing a bright, intelligent, self-reliant, courageous and refreshing variety of the human race." From the seventies until the World War, they raided Europe for culture and clothes. And when Cheltenham girls decided for field hockey rather than frocks, when Girton girls demanded the vote, everyone realized they were imitating American women. Our flashing, high-keyed maidens, as Boyesen said, enlivened dead souls. For they seemed to express a new vitalizing principle in an era that rejected the Virgin and found no coherence in the Dynamo, an age distressed by the Marquis of Queensberry and Huysmans, perplexed by Darwin and Madame Blavatsky. Their special qualities of spirit, Europeans at first believed, could be traced to a kind of moral freedom unique in America — freedom from "the almost pathetic coquetry of the women who must please to live. Perhaps it is only that beside the Old-World women — the product of so many ages of court and salon—she seems so strangely human, so natural, so frank, so New Worldly she is." [2] But as more and more women traveled abroad, as the number of international marriages grew, many Europeans decided that perhaps they had been bemused. The independence of our women was especially pleasing; however, often these people were merely brash. This candid Vassar girl was indeed lovely, her argument against rank and precedence was crisp, informed, clever. But surely that girl from Poughkeepsie was only vulgar, her advice to a peer on how to run the House of Lords, crude. Before long Europeans decided that American women had the best and the worst manners in the world, were shaped by the highest ideals and grossest material values.

There was of course considerable evidence to support the idea of materialism. Ever since 1824 when John Jacob Astor had taken his daughter to Paris in order to marry her to Count Rumpff, a desire for a great marriage had animated the lives of poor princes and decayed democrats. During the seventies and later, such marriages came to have the theatricality and style of coronations. In 1874, as all good Americans know, Jennie Jerome married Lord Randolph Churchill; in 1876, Consuelo Yznaga married the Duke of Manchester; and in 1895 her namesake, Consuelo Vanderbilt, took part in the most famed wedding of the day when she married the Duke of Marlborough. By 1898, Thorstein Veblen was ready to write "The Barbarian Status of Women in America," in which he compared the primitive impulse to marriage with its modern forms in industrial society. "The difficulty of providing wives by feigned capture becomes very great," and marriage by "feigned capture" is invented in order to please predatory men whose status no longer depends on the size of their harems but on the expense of their wives or sons-in-law.[3] Such events and theories and the vulgarity of many American women caused Europeans to decide that most American girls were after all no less predatory than American businessmen. They simply adapted to their sphere the attitudes and procedures which shaped their fathers' or their husbands' lives. Place two men before such women, an appalled Frenchman wrote, "one of whom has but his noble title; and the other distinguished in science, letters . . . there will be no doubt about the young American's choice."[4]

The classic international plot alternates between these two main types of women and as a result helped to fix the world's attention on the best and worst elements in American behavior. The subject interested all writers, the great and the small—Edgar Fawcett and F. Marion Crawford as well as Mrs. Wharton and Henry James—because it quickly displayed both the loveliness and the disorder of the American spirit. There is little reason to speak at length about the heroine who is today still very much with us, the young woman whom everyone admired for bounce and candor.[5] She seemed to represent a sort of animated Statue of Liberty. This heroine has entered our lore and is now the most popular person in musical comedy—"South Pacific," "Miss Liberty."[6] But we have tended to disregard her opposite, the predaceous young woman who seventy-five years ago was almost as famous. At once a form of plunder and herself a plunderer, this heroine first appeared in the 1850's when her fate presented still another illustration of the wages of sin, another argument against American bondage to French morals. Usually, a fashionable American heiress marries a typically corrupt count and eventually finds her way into a tenement on Mulberry Street where she is surrounded by "lesions . . . festering garbage . . . occult dread," doomed to live in a "foul accursed den with an alcoholic husband."[7] The plot was varied to include wrong-minded American men as well.

Later, during the Gilded Age, writers were less fascinated by sin and more preoccupied with the parvenus who tried to crash Society by selling their daughters. "When I issued an order," Mrs. Vanderbilt said about her decision that Consuelo should marry the Duke, nobody discussed it. "I therefore did not beg but ordered her to marry."[8] Mrs. Vanderbilt was not a Chicagoan but the Chicago group of novelists were convinced that her spirit was somehow centered there. Writers such as Henry B. Fuller and Robert Herrick wrote about women in whom money combined with energy developed a code of behavior which was totally unsuited to any place but the remotest frontier. Yet, they said, these women insisted on applying this absurd system in Europe. Herrick has one heroine define a real man as "someone who can make money and make the little men buckle under to you, and the women give you what you want." And the girl in Fuller's "New Wine" urges a similar social and moral economy on her Italian fiancé, a nobleman whose ignorance of the most primitive rules for the successful operation of his estate displeases her. She expects a quick response, too. In America, a woman "had but to be one's lovely self and to declare distinctly one's requirements." Although this kind of girl was not to James's taste, nevertheless he chose similar people for "Miss Gunton of Poughkeepsie" and "The Reverberator." [9] She appears here and there in Howells's fiction too, but she has a unique place in Mrs. Wharton's imagination.

Both Herrick and Fuller were amateurs whose fiction seems to stem from one main source: hatred of Chicago. Fuller's dreams of the Medici, of the quattrocento, of the deep Roman past, held his personal abstract sense of perfect order. Like Edith Wharton's vision of England and France, this was a fantasy. Mrs. Wharton was a more gifted writer and a more intelligent person, however, and when she decided to expose American materialism she learned to see into its center by imitating Henry James. That is, she tried to measure the human loss caused by national barbarity. But partly because she was less humane than James and only a slightly better amateur than Fuller or Herrick, her work shares only a measure of James's distinction and avoids only their most obvious errors. In *The Last Asset*, she chose as the object of scorn no mere silly girl but a woman like Mrs. Vanderbilt, assured, vicious, whose last best asset is her attractive daughter. When a marriage is finally arranged, the occasion itself is not a human event but a dumbshow in which "all the other actors . . . faded . . . beside the dominant figure of Mrs. Newell . . . became mere marionettes pulled . . . by the hidden wires of her intention." [10]

Concerned mainly with the immoral effects of great wealth on American barbarians, Goths whose strength was brute power, Mrs. Wharton was much harsher on women than on men. She saw very clearly how the life of an adventuress like Undine Spragg in *The Custom of the Country* was modeled on her father's business life. And though the father behaved badly, shockingly, at least he reserved his evil for the activities of the Pit or the Street. In contrast, his daughter stayed clear of the jungle but was even more degraded because she was a speculator in another kind of bond, in men. And the novel expresses its meaning through her many marriages, which occur in Indiana, New York City, France. Married to Ralph Marvell, she turns this dignified and honest man, who "now and then gets ten dollars for his poetry," into a suicide. Next in line is Raymond de Chelles, a French nobleman of "simplicity and intelligence" who mistakes Undine for a beautiful candid American girl. But of course she hasn't inherited the dream of all the ages, merely its materials—energy and ambition and limitless egoism. This marriage bores her because she cannot adapt herself to the role required of "the ladies of the line of Chelles," who sit "at their needlework on the terrace." She leaves to marry Elmer Moffatt and enter her proper arena, "the New York Nouveau Luxe." Elmer and Undine—their very names evoke Mrs. Wharton's disgust—prey on the world, rigging its markets and corrupting its honor; they compose the best Society in the New World.[11] Unlike European society where "painters and poets and novelists and men of science . . . were as sought after as Dukes," their circle has no sense of purpose or duty or place, no respect for tradition or mind. For the very image which Proust was shortly to expunge filled Mrs. Wharton's golden dreams. Where he saw an inordinately complex game in which only the pawns remained, she visualized "an intensely social race in a setting of immemorial manners." [12]

James was clearer-minded about and more patient with his countrymen. When he turned his attention to this subject he preferred not to linger over its rawest occasions and specimens but to lay bare the deepest evil in the people of highest polish. He recognized these women as victims of their society, their parents; of a national stupidity in the way of the world which did not insulate them against the worst effects of certain European customs. Rootless persons who hyphenated their surnames and invented coats of arms were disjoined from the meaning of American life and as a result they degraded themselves, their country, and their humanity. But they were merely gross versions of people like "Louisa Pallant" or Christina Light of *Roderick Hudson*, girls schooled in malice by the worldliest of mothers. All slip past the point where regeneration and love are possible and suffer the most terrible of all losses: waste of life. Christina, tutored by her mother in pretense and envy, knows that her marriage to the Prince is the glittering moment for which since birth she's been trained. Materialism of whatever society, James said, like American gentility, violates love hence corrodes life. It can be overcome only by some act of heroism, an act based in self-recognition and judgment: hence Christina renounces Hudson and for his good dooms herself to the Prince. Similarly, Mrs. Pallant warns off the best kind of American suitor, the kind of man she had hoped her daughter would marry, because the girl would ruin him. What we are left with is deep respect for the martyr and — as in the instance of genteel prudery — an overwhelming sense of the absurdity and horror of such waste.

In one very elaborate novel, *The Wings of the Dove*, he molded his own ideas, and those that customarily informed this plot, into new forms which simultaneously enabled him to write an allegory, a tragedy. He showed how Europeans, too, despite their high civilization, could be ruined by a crudeness no less gross than the American. Ruin is indeed the more terrible because the more subtle, the waste of life more cruel precisely because these people do not recognize, till too late, that they had rejected the richest imaginable kind of existence, offered them by the heroine, Milly Theale. And she is the most beautiful being the American moral imagination could conceive. "I had from far back," James wrote in the Preface to this novel, "projected a certain sort of young American as more the 'heir of all the ages' than any other young person whatever."[13] Despite James's avowed design — to reanimate the American sentiment of sex — he reserved a very grave respect, in certain women, for the stateliest national maxims. And Milly is the saintliest of possible women in a novel where James combined his praise and dispraise of the idea of innocence in order to expose a form of European greed far deadlier than our own.

As in all tragedies, the source of this heroine's distinction is also the sign of her doom: rich, young, kind, wise, Milly has everything except health. She suffers some sort of ineffable disease and, in search of a cure, she goes abroad where she is implicated in the maneuverings of two burnished Europeans, Kate Croy and Merton Densher. They plot to get her money when she dies. Their plan works; Milly comes to love Densher until one of her other suitors informs her of the nasty scheme. She dies but leaves her money to the pair anyway. As a result they are not merely shamed—they are deracinated, their lives are turned upside down. "We shall never again be as we were," Kate tells Densher. He can no longer touch the money because Milly has destroyed his passion for cash. "Her memory's your love." "You *want* no other."[14]

What happened to Densher is not simply that he lost the will to live a well-appointed life but that he learned from Milly the highest meanings of love. Only an American woman—a most purely genteel, bodiless American lady—can serve as a symbol of absolute love, James said, of the human impulse to achieve perfection on earth. Brought into existence by the highest-minded society in history, she represents its hope and its conscience, its effort to establish a system in which men will live justly and love mercy. Unlike Christina Light, Milly is less a Christian than a Swedenborgian martyr; like Christina, she is also a human being who wants love. She prefers to live not to die and she wants Densher as her husband far more than she wants sainthood. Because Milly is not metaphorically angelic, however, but is virtually an angel, she is foredoomed. For she can live only through love, only by "taking full in the face the whole assault of life," only by giving herself absolutely. And the only kind of love that can sustain her is not possible in our world.

This mine, James insisted that we understand, "but needed working and would certainly yield a treasure." The irony implicit in the metaphor, in its sexual imagery, refers to Densher's decision to take the money merely, to exploit her latent passion, but not to see in both an analogue of the inexhaustible riches of the spirit. This man of everyday virtue is precisely the sort of person Milly needs because the duty of this perfectly pure woman is to raise human love to her special order of intensity and goodness: to make human passion something other than itself. And human love, as Kate and Densher are designed to show, involves evil, is inextricable from bodies, passions, dollars. Milly's nameless, tragic disease, then, paradoxically, is absolute goodness: she cannot join flesh and spirit in a balance like that of Mary Garland in *Roderick Hudson* who "looked like a Medusa . . . crowned with the tremor of dove's wings." Milly cannot, as Maggie Verver discovers she must, combine the qualities of a nun with those of a nymph in order to live with her husband in this world. Superbly unviable, she does not have and cannot ever acquire that unique combination of purity and passion, perfection and imperfection, which defines the human condition and makes love and human intercourse possible in this life. Thus James mined the vein of materialism inherent in the international plot, struck another—embedded in the cult of gentility—then exploited both in order to say that each could yield a great prize.

But he had not reached bedrock. Like his associates, he chose this strategy as a good way to imply what was best and worst in American women and civilization. He revealed the distortion of certain American values and the other-worldliness of some of this nation's aims. Americans were at their worst when they came to Europe equipped only with the values of business and then superimposed on these precisely that kind of European glitter which, in *The Golden Bowl*, he called gilt over cracked glass. But they were at their best when they combined, as he wrote in a letter to his brother William, moral spontaneity and intellectual grace. Yet James was unsatisfied by this rather meager use of a striking method, extraordinary because it allowed him to relate the inner lives of his heroines to the whole life of society.

Despite the esteem he felt for Milly he set himself the task, within the structure of this plot, of understanding why American women were so poorly equipped to take the whole assault of life. The first intimations had come to him during a trip to Rome in the fall of 1877, and had begun to coalesce later that spring when he sat down to write *Daisy Miller*. Those were the days when hosts of American girls invaded the Continent and any one of them might have inspired James, any one might have picked up "a good-looking Roman of vague identity" and "all innocently, all serenely exhibited and introduced" him until Society made her realize that such a man was not acceptable. This incident, reported by a friend in Rome as having actually occurred during the previous winter, seemed to express American girlish innocence.

Coincidentally, there is a diary written by precisely this sort of young woman, *Julia Newberry's Diary*, which illustrates the deep interpenetration of James's art and real life. Had James read the diary he would have realized how accurately he knew Julia, her class, and her quality. Her father, Walter L. Newberry, in the sixties had made a fortune in Chicago real estate, established his family in Society, endowed the present Newberry Library, and himself had become a central figure in the public life of the City. Julia's own participation in the great world dates from 1870; her trips to Europe prefigure similar journeys of many other young women. Indeed, she is the prototype of the lively, candid, patriotic American girl. What was extraordinary in 1869 became cliché ten years later, for she was one of the first to say shocking things to her staid hosts. "If Paris surrenders I shall be utterly crestfallen . . . and if the Parisians haven't sufficient patriotism to remain united while the enemy is at their gates, they deserve the contempt of everyone." This was the unique American style with which our girls established their reputation for forthright good sense. And her opinion of an ideal American girl reads like Howells's: girls must be "bright, clever, independent and ambitious," full of "fun, humor, sarcasm, and enthusiasm." Julia might have added irreverence—the key quality in everybody's heroine—a disrespect for even the most sacred cow. She says that Johann Strauss, when she met him, "acted like a monkey"; that a friend looked horrid, "just like the Prince of Wales"; that General Phil Sheridan, whose reputation at that moment was very high indeed, had "a nice foot, and good manners and an Irish accent." He made, she says, a great many sweet speeches, "none of which were very original." Furthermore, she was at once demure and responsive. Describing a conversation begun by a stranger, an Englishman, she wrote: "I never talk to strangers but . . . I answer civilly enough . . . we discuss fifty different subjects . . . & it was quite romantic to be talking to him for an hour or so." Doubtless Julia was as virtuous a young woman as it was possible to find but an English gentleman would have been disinclined to begin a conversation of this sort with a British girl of his class.[15]

Had James known Julia, he would have placed her immediately. But he could not have known her because, like Daisy, she died in Rome of what was called an inflammation of the throat, and was buried there on April 4, 1876. A formal notice of her death was printed and circulated, however, and may have been available to James himself when he arrived in that city the following year. Surely, it had been available to the friend who told him the anecdote that set him to work on the novel. I suspect that James never admitted he had heard about Julia because he wanted to protect her, and himself, against his American public, outraged because it claimed that the novel derogated American women. But the gossipy colony in Rome—in which James dined—could scarcely have forgotten the deaths of the two Newberry girls (Julia's sister had died the year before Julia died). Two very rich, cultivated, young, American, fatherless girls, whose home had been lost in the Chicago fire, had died abroad—striking events which must have provided the stuff of endless gossip. Furthermore, Mrs. Newberry took an apartment in Paris and never returned to America. This was exactly the kind of situation James prized most.

Whether or not the story of Julia's fate, along with that other anecdote he admitted having heard, inspired James, the important thing is the way *Daisy Miller* implies the grand theme and great quest of his career, finally dramatized in *The Golden Bowl*: what elements compose an ideal woman, an ideal marriage, not of North and South or East and West but of America and Europe? For Rome was James's peak in Darien quite as Rome was the scene of Adam

Verver's extraordinary self-discovery. The glittering Prince Amerigo, too, is surely transmuted out of the lead which composed Giovanelli, Daisy's escort. Thus *Daisy Miller*—not "An International Episode" or "Pandora" or even *The Wings of the Dove*—announces the central motifs of James's imagination, their incorporation in the classic international plot.

The plot turns on one dramatic action: in Europe with her mother and brother, Daisy does not know how to behave. She has been reared to do as she pleases and as a result does not know the old distinction between freedom and license. Her training has made her charmingly independent but stubborn. And her resistance both to fetters and to new ideas at once enlivens and ruins her. Though it has made her warm-hearted, singularly honest and trusting, it does not allow her to obey a European code which is rooted in cynicism, not honor. She permits an Italian dancing master to escort her, unchaperoned, about Rome, and this behavior confuses Europeans who cannot tell if she is bad or stupid. Still insisting upon personal freedom, she allows Giovanelli to take her into the Coliseum where exposure to malaria kills her. In James's mind, the irony of Daisy's behavior is her refusal to accept a code of manners worse than her own: this decision expresses her American courage to reject the opinion of nasty minds—what Howells called her angelic incapacity to "behave as discreetly as worse people."[16] Daisy is very much like Euphemia in "Madame de Mauves," an American girl whose imperturbable virtue drives her normal, pleasant, French, sensualist-husband to suicide. He had accepted the manners of his society and lived apart from his wife, while Euphemia lived in soundless virtue. Finally, he comes to admire her but she is so inordinately pure that she will not return a sinful man's love. Thus James, with tongue in cheek, showed how pointless is this superb American gentility which destroys the very things it seeks to preserve. Daisy kills only herself.

James's sexual imagination is subtle indeed and we should be unable to trace its place in this story had not other writers chosen for similar effect its central imagery. For James insists that Daisy is "most innocent," that she is merely flirting with Giovanelli, inappropriately but naively. She may be flirting, James says, but "Mr. Giovanelli is not; he means something else." We can recreate the effect of that scene in the Coliseum upon James's outraged audience if we recall Frank R. Stockton's famous parable, "The Lady or the Tiger?" Referring to the common sport in the Coliseum during its heyday, Stockton posed a dilemma: will the Roman lover choose the right door and open it to discover the lady, his love, or will he choose wrong and be devoured by a tiger? Howells chose similar terms for one of his heroines who, though "sylvan," is also much like "that black leopard up there in Central Park": "fierce, flashing, feline." His audience took sylvan to mean womanly, hence virtuous; feline to mean sexual, hence dangerous.

What Stockton allegorized for his generation is the abiding question, is sex delightful or devouring, beneficent or consuming, good or evil? When James caused the unacceptable Giovanelli to take Daisy to that "fatal place," he evoked images of license and not merely of girlish freedom. This effect was guaranteed, too, by their conversation. She observes of one of the statues that "he looks at us as one of the old lions or tigers may have looked at the Christian martyrs." Giovanelli says, "He will have to take me first; you will serve for dessert." A moment later, "in a strange little tone," Daisy replies, "I don't care . . . whether I have Roman fever or not." Lest we miss the effect of this banter, James causes Winterbourne, his spokesman, to overhear the conversation and decide—till this moment he had defended Daisy against criticism—that "she was a young lady whom a gentleman need no longer be at pains to respect."[17] For Daisy has a totally inaccurate idea of the power of sex not only on Giovanelli and all cynical Europeans but mainly on herself. Later, Giovanelli attests her innocence: they had not been lovers. But James hit on this elaborately indirect way of saying something more serious than calling Daisy immoral. Clearly, she isn't immoral—she is ignorant; she's not simply innocent—she is infantile and she childishly throws away her life. She plays with the tiger of passion as if the beast were jocular, American. Relying on the erotic myth of Europe, as in *The Bostonians* he was to rely on the erotic myth of the South, James hoped to intimate his idea yet retain his audience. In both novels, of course, he failed. And though he denied all accusations, to my mind none of his replies is convincing.[18]

Other writers, incidentally, shared James's opinion but were defter at hiding — from themselves and their readers — the radical meaning of their ideas. The heroine of "An American Beauty" is severely criticized because she doesn't even have a body to speak of. She was "almost ethereal in form, or as her detractors would have said, she was extremely thin." This "lovely wax doll," did nothing all day but sit in a lawn chair dressed in a "sublimated" tennis costume, fiddling with "her dress and its ornaments." This bodiless girl, the brightest ornament of American gentility, is admired by an earl who is finally persuaded against marriage by his more perspicuous family.[19] She may have a fortune in hardware, they say, but is herself composed of the brittlest metal. Thus magazine fiction made criticism acceptable.

Not until much later was society prepared to accept Mrs. Wharton's less euphemized opinion of American women. For if James was severe, she was severer still and in *The Age of Innocence* she said flatly that sweet little girls cannot fulfill their destiny because they haven't the slightest idea how to fulfill themselves. Their proud innocence and purity were "artificial," "factitious," cunningly manufactured by a "conspiracy of mothers and aunts" and designed to create bovine young women with a talent for "wifely adoration." She much preferred the kind of girl who replaces "bounce and bang" with a "fineness of perception" rooted in the remotest "depths of initiation."[20] These were of course exactly the effects on Chad Newsome, in *The Ambassadors*, of his affair with Madame de Vionnet. She turns Chad from a New England provincial into a "man of the world," a man "marked out by women." As a result of his liaison with this superb Frenchwoman — of living, according to his mother, in sin — Chad is made "actually smooth," has been put into a "firm mould and turned successfully out." Initiation into the mysteries of love has "cleared his eyes and settled his colour and polished his fine square teeth . . . toned his voice, established his accent . . . He had formerly with a great deal of action expressed very little; and now he expressed whatever was necessary with almost none at all." [21] Until James wrote *The Golden Bowl* he felt easier saying these things about a man. But he and Mrs. Wharton held a common view of the benign influence of "Europe"—sexual experience—on all innocent Americans.[22] The wages of sin were life.

Unless American women were taught to recognize this truth, were trained in this new school, they would never succeed in transvaluing values. As a novelist committed to the Lincolnian ideal, to the messianic hope, James never forswore his own hope that two beautiful, self-assured human beings would achieve a great marriage in which the two great civilizations would be joined. But as a realist of the imagination, he understood that most women would live sad, incomplete, noble, un-Europeanized lives. This is Isabel Archer's condition, and in *The Portrait of a Lady* he showed how one of the loveliest of women, a person who combines "inflated ideals" with "meagre knowledge," is really foredoomed. Shaw, in his Preface to *Heartbreak House*, said that cultivated leisured Europe before the War was a vacuum filled with sex. James thrusts Isabel into this vacuum: he sends her to Europe and almost immediately burdens her with the task of choosing a husband.

Untutored in the discipline of passion, she is at a loss how to proceed. And as soon as opportunities for decision occur, she begins to err. She rejects Lord Warburton, the very best candidate: he is a true aristocrat because he knows, respects, and judges his traditions. His notion of the aristocratic life was simply the union "of great knowledge with great liberty; the knowledge would give one a sense of duty, and the liberty a sense of enjoyment." But Isabel turns her back on the best Europe can provide quite as she refuses the best that America alone can create, Caspar Goodwood, "a straight young man from Boston." She decides on Gilbert Osmond whom she sees as a very lonely, a very cultivated, and a very honest man. Actually, Osmond is a "sterile dilettante" and fortune hunter. Isabel cannot see that he is only an imitation of the real thing—like Ward McAllister, Osmond had an "immense esteem for tradition" though no one knew "from what source he derived his traditions." She is the victim of a plot hatched by a schemer and a voluptuary — James reminds us of Machiavelli and Vittoria Colonna — Osmond and the mother of his child, Madame Merle, Americans corrupted by European sensualism. Because she has been reared in a place where sex is not supposed to help mold decisions, she is unable to distinguish among choices which involve the application of its force.

Once Isabel has been initiated, however, she does understand herself. Awareness occurs in the moment when she rediscovers Caspar, the man who had been available from the first. Goodwood had seemed merely dull because he had worshiped her according to good American fashion. But finally he declares his mind with a freedom unlikely in America — with the same clean intensity that distinguished Moody's Steve Ghent. And Isabel discovers "that she had never been loved before . . . This was the hot wind of the desert . . . It wrapped her about; it lifted her off her feet while the very taste of it, as of something potent, acrid and strange forced open her set teeth." [23] After long ignorance and pain two proper Americans, equipped by nature but not by tradition, discover and recognize the exhilaration and power of passion. The discovery comes too late, of course: Isabel is resigned to being Osmond's wife. What it reveals is James's hope that some day it will not come too late.

This plot appeared at about the time when international marriages became popular, and as these grew more and more dazzling and elaborate, it too accrued larger and larger intricacy. Destiny's darling, people everywhere began to realize, very often became merely the plaything of fortune, herself a huntress or a victim of a hunter of fortune. And by the end of the century, the whole matter was virtually reserved for Henry James who, Howells wrote, may not have been the "inventor of the international novel" but who was without question the inventor of "the international American girl." [24] Unlike the creatures in popular fiction, his heroines were not designed to please an indefatigable national delight in the American social conquest of Europe. For he saw in the international theme still another subject through which he could expose the inner lives of American women. Then he decided that the qualities which defined the very best feminine spirit were precious but ineffective in an undiscriminating world. And he committed himself to the principle for which Henry Adams spoke: "a sex-conscious Daisy Miller might conquer the earth."[25] Believing that American society denied its women the most fertile kinds of consciousness and, instead, furnished pieties that sensitized the soul but tortured the flesh, James created the Europeanized American girl. She served best as a symbol of international and universal harmony because she alone achieved inner harmony, a balance of initiation and innocence.

He reserved his highest praise, therefore, for Maggie Verver, not Milly Theale—for the women who survived and flourished because they harmonized body and spirit. Only these women could fulfill their destiny, for they alone were able to reform Europe and remold America. Long after this was established as the Jamesian vision of the New Jerusalem, the general public was willing to share his opinion though it chose less convincing reasons. Led by the editors of family magazines, society admired most of all the girl who "has been abroad from her childhood and has learned . . . the language . . . and manners of other countries. She has within her just a suggestion of independence and girlish freedom which our women enjoy at home . . . and it gives her a modest manner and a graceful piquancy possessed by no other girl in the world. Miss Halldeman of Dresden . . . came originally from Leavenworth, Kansas."[26]

But James did not sentimentalize his idea nor was he satisfied with this image. There was one unanswered, pressing question: why was only a certain kind of American woman able to balance passion and romance—achieve that inner harmony? He decided that the secret of her quality was not simply a matter of geography or history or Europeanization but was contained in biography. James was not the first to deduce that the essential clues to her nature were to be found in her family, but he was the only American artist who penetrated and understood its whole force.

♀

The spirit of Myrrha

"DEAR MISS DIX: It is a source of great regret to me that I am not as close to my father as other girls are to their fathers. How can I remedy this situation?

ANSWER: . . . He probably has the same feeling as you have, but just doesn't know how to get closer to you. A father-daughter relationship can be one of the most beautiful things in life."

"That is the ancient spirit of Myrrha who was devoted to her father beyond the bounds of lawful love."

ALL American writers in the nineteenth century, even those who each month in the ladies' magazines flattered the feminine audience, share one notable commitment. Uninterested in the sheer surface of a thing, they felt compelled to uncover the sources of human motive and behavior. Those Western novelists, for example, who located a woman's violence in the wildness of her region and the savagery of her family, drew these conclusions in an effort to pierce the mystery of her nature. The impulse was rooted in the folk remark, "I want to know!" The expression was imprecise — it denoted awe, amazement, and it connoted society's conviction that knowledge however unsystematic was somehow crucial: the printer's devil and Yankee pedlar had a proverb or a patch to solve every problem. Too, the remark carries the flavor of the earliest time when in the vast new country a nervous people tried to identify strangers by the cut of their cloth, the tiny signs of origin and attitude, in order to distinguish between enemies and friends.[1]

Even in the time when an austere morality disciplined art and life, therefore, literature did its work in a characteristically American fashion. It was D. H. Lawrence who first saw, Lionel Trilling has said, that "American literature of the great age was . . . more profound than the French or English in that it went deeper into the unconscious life of society."[2] Outside America a novelist's duty required that personality be discovered in milieu and defined by certain qualities of caste: a man does this or that because elder sons are predictable. James was aware of this distinction and he was proud of the American talent for searching out the deep and hidden stuff behind motive. At the moment when he admired Trollope's familiarity with "all sorts and conditions of men, with the business of life, with affairs . . . with every component part of the ancient fabric of English society"—even then he claimed that Trollope at his most persuasive was broad. But American writers were deft at doing what Trollope evaded, examining and mastering "all the springs" of the delicate human organism and particularly that most "complicated being," the American girl.[3] American literature, having set out to learn all that it could about this alluring person, decided that what distinguished her was a certain unique combination of sex and innocence, and this it attributed to the influences of geography, of a national respect for vital, healthy people, and of Europe. Then it made an impressive discovery. At bottom, this new harmony in the feminine soul existed only when a girl felt some special affection for her father.

We know, of course, that family life in the last century was hardly serene. At its best, life was comfortable, graceful. But unfortunately people more often suffered than pleased one another. And literature is a kind of dialogue in which one group delicately and at times majestically condemns another group for causing grievances which nowadays we consider very serious indeed. This situation is contained in two classic plots in which mothers and sons are joined in an allegiance against fathers and daughters. In an early form the subject appeared in a story about a young bride who is troubled by the prospect of moving into her husband's home. She knows that his mother cannot yield traditional duties and privileges to an intruder. When she demands her husband's support he reminds her that his mother has "so long been the mistress of my home" that it is too much to expect that she "should heartily rejoice in my marriage." Piqued, the girl replies that he is the "best judge which is most necessary to your happiness — mother or wife." His advice — patience — is exasperating and she leaves. But we realize that she has behaved improperly; she has been inhospitable, selfish, petulant, and immoral. Finally she understands that her husband is not only guiltless but also truly honorable — "if he had given up his mother, even for my sake, I must inevitably have loved him less." True manliness requires that loyalty to a mother supersede loyalty to a wife and our heroine discerns this because she has been trained in what the writers of the day believed was a first-rate school. "Mother died so long ago that I only cherished a memory . . . Since her death I had been my father's all, as he had been mine." This experience qualified our heroine for marriage with the physician who attended her physician-father during his last illness. "Because I knew what you were as a daughter," he congratulates her when she admits her error, "I knew I could trust my happiness without fear in your hands." His discernment is also a quality of *his* breeding — his experience complements hers: "My father died when I was a year old . . . [Mother] brought me up and gave me every advantage."[4] A woman's best preparation for marriage, this story says, is her affinity with her father; a man's is the tie that binds him to mother. Marriage is best when it joins persons who are properly, indeed peculiarly, filial. Much later, when Henry James decided to search out the heart of the matter in *The Golden Bowl*, he chose a daughter who was "passionately filial" and a father who was "peculiarly paternal."

James's opinion as well as the situation that underlies this story is duplicated in the many tales where an alliance between a father and his daughter does not complement but instead conflicts with an alliance between a mother and her son. When the girl is especially admirable, ordinarily she is far more charming than her mother who, in turn, is derogated by her husband. And if the daughter is loyal to her father, her brother's allegiance is to his mother; if she is patriotic, he is a foppish anglophile. In a novel by Henry B. Fuller, *With the Procession*, Truesdale is the darling of his "sapless" mother; he writes and paints and dines, believing himself to set an example of high fashion. Jane, the daughter, is the only one "who really loves me," her father thinks; she has been "never a trial, never a disappointment — nothing but a comfort." After his death, she is inconsolable until she finds a man who "filled measurably" her father's idea of a suitable husband. In *An Ambitious Woman*, Edgar Fawcett described a heroine's mother as vulgar and stupid, her father as an Englishman of good breeding fallen from his former station. The girl "bore a striking resemblance to her father . . . she possessed his sloping delicacy of visage, and his erect though slender frame." [5]

Physical resemblance, incidentally, was a common way to signify alignments. "This one daughter," H. H. Boyesen said in *The Light of Her Countenance*, who resembled her father "as much as a woman can resemble a man without loss of charm, had been his pet and dearest companion from her earliest years . . . her mother . . . was amiable and commonplace." [6] And in Edith Wharton's Old New York series, *False Dawn* is about a gentle son who is like his gentle mother; sent abroad to buy Italian old masters for his father's collection, he returns with the work of Italian primitives. Refusing to conform to his father's idea of masculinity — a real man is a businessman — and of art, he is disinherited. He achieves a kind of sainthood as a patron of the arts who shows the work of great but unknown artists. Actual sainthood occurs in Howells's *A Hazard of New Fortunes* where Conrad Dryfoos, whose vulgar, pious, unambitious mother was raised by Dunkards, disappoints his millionaire father by wanting to be a preacher. He is killed interceding in a strike. It was Howells, too, who wondered why "we always leave the mother out . . . when we sum up hereditary tendencies." [7]

Howells's wonder may have been authentic but probably he had an opinion on the matter. For American social history itself had long provided numerous occasions of this kind and Howells was a man on whom nothing was lost. It was a fact of history that our most distinguished as well as our most disabled women had been somehow especially favored by their fathers and themselves had formed a nearly unshakable attachment to these men. In the beginning, this attachment was the result of a unique American conviction that women were not frivolous by nature; environment rendered them inept. This belief helped women to establish their right to education — it underscored the argument that well-taught women would help to preserve the Republic and its values, urged in 1787 by Benjamin Rush — and was introduced without publicity into many families where girls were given rigorous training by their parents. Usually, the father took over the conduct or chose the method of the girl's education. Aaron Burr, for example, gave the legendary Theodosia a classical training virtually in order to prove that a woman properly led could distinguish herself. His elaborate concern bred a very intense intimacy which was exaggerated when her mother died and she became, at fourteen, his hostess. Their affection sets in relief similar "marriages" that were to follow. "You appear to me so superior, so elevated above other men," she wrote to him during his exile, "I contemplate you with such a strange mixture of humility, admiration, reverence, love, and pride, that very little superstition would be necessary to make me worship you as a superior being . . . I had rather not live than not be the daughter of such a man."[8] Not only do these remarks set a tone which continues even in our day but also they may well help to explain the fate of Henry Adams's wife, Marian Hooper, whom James placed alongside his cousin, Minny Temple, in the first rank of American women. Adams himself chose an affection of this kind for his novel, *Esther*. And his wife decided for suicide shortly after her father died in 1885. "There had always been a tender relationship between them," says a specialist in Adams's affairs, Harold Dean Cater, "each leaning on the other . . . She was his youngest daughter, motherless since she was five, and had never left home until she married at the age of twenty-eight."[9] Theodosia's career foreshadows, too, that of Kate Chase Sprague, the daughter of Lincoln's Secretary of the Treasury Salmon P. Chase. After her stepmother's death, she became her father's hostess in the Governor's mansion in Columbus, where Howells admired her beauty and vivacity. She was sixteen. Later, her marriage to Senator Sprague of Rhode Island was part of her plan to achieve the presidency for her father. The plan was disastrous but this did not shake her allegiance. Before the marriage ended in scandal and divorce, Kate set up apartments for Chase in Sprague's house—quite as Adam Verver in *The Golden Bowl* maintains space for Maggie. "How I do love you, my darling," Chase wrote to her, "My whole heart seems to go out towards you . . . and tears come to my eyes."[10]

Not all girls found a common fate but the women of largest reputation in the last century shared a common experience. Susan B. Anthony's father, read out of meeting for allowing dancing in his house, married a girl his parents disapproved of and taught his own children. Lucretia Mott's father, a democrat whose views were opposed by his wife, insisted that Lucretia be sent to a public school where she would acquire "democratic sympathies." Like many girls in fiction she married her father's business partner; later she became Hicksite Quaker when the group itself was suspect. Another feminist, Mrs. M. J. Gage, was taught the liberal arts at home by her father, a man who made his home a center for the avant garde. Elizabeth Cady Stanton studied law at home with hers; Margaret Fuller said that her father taught her as much as he knew then sent her to school until he no longer could afford the cost.[11] A main result of this alliance, apparently, was the creation of able women who took on the job of reform. And when the compact lost its high sanction, what remained was the custom of affinity and its resonance in the feminine soul.

This is the special quality in the American domestic situation that literature chose to exploit. Returning to our heroines, we discover that the most impressive girls have an intense affection for their fathers. The alliance between them is marked by a "subtile sentiment," as Thomas Bailey Aldrich claimed, that "cannot exist in the case of mother and daughter, or . . . of son and mother." It is the crucial fact of the heroine's biography. The writers do not use it casually or frivolously and instead choose this affinity when they are intent on establishing the quality of her sensibility, the charm of her person, the source of her talent in love. From the moment when this attachment first appears in fiction, the girl's lover and an admiring audience realize that a woman of this kind makes the best wife. "I recommend to all my young friends who wish to be well-off in this life," one young man advises, "to marry a girl whose Papa is likely to have an *organic affection*."[12]

The prime purpose of this affinity, then, was to intimate a woman's sexual address—to exaggerate it by presenting as her foil the prototypical genteel female who is as innocent of evil as a child. Usually this angelic person has no father at all, merely a poor widowed mother. But the girl who is desirable and truly nubile is given an alternate biography. Often she is an only daughter who "associated with her father and two brothers from early childhood, partook of their spirit most cordially—a spirit which by nature and education embraced broad grounds." This remark refers to a girl of special candor and verve when neither was fashionable. "When girls say that they do not like caresses from any man," she informs her lover, "they do not speak the truth." "Too many women from a false notion of delicacy, or a special fear" deny that "warm personal regard" which even the "purest women sometimes . . . feel." Despite her candor, her daring, her frank joy in sex, this girl is not called a temptress or a coquette—the common epithets for bold and attractive women. She is merely more desirable than the angelic female whose soul was "lovely with a delicate flowerlike grace and bloom"—in the vocabulary of the day, she is "more companionable," more alert to the "magnetism," the "passionate power" of the man she loves.[13]

Genteel writers did not specify why paternal influence somehow involved education in sex. Indeed their chief aim was to idealize the affection between a tender daughter and a solicitous father in order to please a sentimental society. Placing a girl within her father's orbit was first of all good politics and only incidentally acute psychology. Yet the relation provided a kind of shorthand through which the two most perplexing qualities in a woman's character—her virtue and her accessibility—were rendered graphic: it guaranteed her lure and did not discredit her honor. From midcentury on, therefore, genteel fiction justified sex by disclosing its place in the process in which even the purest women were bred; and it accomplishd this feat by remaining within the limits of a very rigid code based in a very exacting moral imagination.

Even the most commonplace writers of the day came to rely on this convention. Strikingly, it received first real fame when one of the most orthodox, Thomas Bailey Aldrich, composed his little fantasy, *Marjorie Daw*. Cast in the form of a bundle of letters between two young men, the tale places Ned at the seaside attending an ailing father and Jack in bed brooding about his broken leg. The central action is begun when Jack's doctor writes Ned and says something must be done to take Jack's mind off his leg — he is dangerously close to melancholia. In order to lure Jack back to life Ned invents a Galatea — he pretends that there is a pure and exciting young woman at the resort to whom he constantly speaks of his friend. In the first letter Ned says that there is little to write about because he is at a remote place, else he would fill Jack's imagination with "groups of sea-goddesses . . . you should have Aphrodite in morning wrapper, in evening costume, and in her prettiest bathing suit." In lieu of real girls, therefore, Ned conceives the genteel gentleman's dream lady, Marjorie Daw, who is "eighteen, and has golden hair, and dark eyes and an emerald-colored illusion dress . . . All this splendor goes into that hammock and sways there." Pretending that he contrived to meet her, he describes conversations of which Jack is the sole subject. And within a week he reports that "she has all but confessed her interest in you." At first Jack is unresponsive but Ned artfully rouses him from torpor to passion — indeed what Aldrich succeeded in composing is a kind of genteel pornography which he held within the limit of decency by mixing sensuality with cant. Creating what his audience must have recognized as a sexual fantasy, he justified his effort by saying that his story has the serious purpose of reanimating his hero's will to live — use venery for reasons of health, Ben Franklin had said.

Eventually, Jack rises from bed and wires that he is coming to claim this splendid girl. Ned must confess there is no Marjorie Daw — that she seesaws only in the imagination. It is the letter that turned the trick, therefore, the remark which finally propelled Jack from bed, which interests us. Ned had begun by describing a visit to Marjorie's house, and in order to recreate a vision of her beauty he reported her special affection for her widowed father. Her attendance upon us was charming, Ned says, "she brought cigars and lighted the tapers with her own delicate fingers, in the most enchanting fashion."

> It was easy to see that the old Colonel worshipped her, and she him. I think the relationship between an elderly father and a daughter just blooming into womanhood the most beautiful possible. There is in it a subtile sentiment that cannot exist in the case of mother and daughter, or that of son and mother.

But, he concludes, "this is getting into deep water." And he ends the letter saying, "We talked about the weather—and you!"[14] This is the last straw and Jack leaves his sickbed.

The girl who beautifully and innocently lighted her father's cigar figured in the American imagination as a person who somehow held the torch of experience but was untouched by its heat. She embodied an excellent solution to the old problem: What is the origin of and what is the proper response to a good woman's sexual attraction? Deciding that the whole matter is rooted in innocent but intense affection between peculiarly paternal men and passionately filial women, literature answered the question to its own satisfaction, fulfilled its drive to expose the inner life of its heroines, represented an affinity which everyone recognized, and presented to society a woman whom everybody admired.

The success of this formula, however, lay in a writer's delicacy and ingenuity. Genteel literature is, after all, a kind of history of ingenuity, delicacy, and obsession. Artists who were encouraged to engage the question of love but denied the right to speak out were forced to turn to symbolism. One of their best discoveries is the symbolism of gold. Perhaps it is more accurate to say rediscovery, for Ernest Jones's essay on the symbolic uses of salt remarks that gold as an image of fertilization is a favorite theme in mythology. Its best known instance is that of Danaë being impregnated by a shower of golden rain. Doubtless we are more familiar with Shakespeare's use of similar images throughout *Othello* and *The Merchant of Venice*, or in the poem where Venus tries to seduce Adonis, saying, "Gold that's put to use more gold begets." We recall, too, that the favorite metaphor describing an American heroine called her the heiress of all the ages. She was a person of metaphor indeed, but in fact she was usually very rich. And most often her wealth was provided by her father. History supplied the symbolism, therefore, and the national economic consciousness supplied the ground of a very useful way to describe the nature and source of an ideal woman's richest endowment. As the imagery unfolds we realize that a girl's opulence is in effect interest on the fund she stores with her father — her husband is forever in debt to his father-in-law. And if a girl — much like the widow's angelic child — turns out to be too good, too pure, too beautiful to live, ordinarily she dies a spinster sapped by sacrifices to a family impoverished by her father.

Speculating on the origins of this formulation, I suspect that its first notable appearance occurs in Hawthorne's version of the Midas-legend, written in *The Wonder-Book*. Hawthorne turned Ovid's legend into a statement about American habits quite as its companion piece, "Rappaccini's Daughter," though placed in exotic, erotic Italy, is an indirect statement of the same subject. Together, the stories present two sides of a coin — one relates the maleficent force of a father upon his daughter, the other records the distinction he confers. "Once upon a time there lived a very rich man, and a king besides, whose name was Midas; and he had a little daughter, whom nobody but myself ever heard of, and whose name I either never knew, or have entirely forgotten. So . . . I choose to call her Marygold." Midas was fonder of gold than of anything, Hawthorne continues, but he loved his daughter even more: "the more Midas loved his daughter, the more did he desire and seek for wealth." His greed, like Rappaccini's science, is aimed at providing his daughter the best stuff of life: he wanted "to bequeath to her the immensest pile of yellow, glistening coin, that had ever been heaped together." Both men, therefore, wish to endow their daughters with great power magically got. That Hawthorne conceived them as a pair is implied, too, in Midas's "great taste for flowers." Before he had become fascinated by gold, "he had planted a garden, in which grew the biggest and beautifullest and sweetest roses that any mortal ever saw or smelt." We recognize Hawthorne's intention: using two metaphors jointly, he presented Midas as a man of passion. Indeed, Midas is a man of grave appetite which unintentionally he directs at his daughter: his kiss turns her into a golden statue. But he honestly loves her and is therefore not depraved — he begs the mysterious stranger to cleanse his soul. This person perceives that Midas's heart "has not been entirely changed from flesh to gold" and Midas is allowed to immerse himself in a river. He plunged and "a cold, hard, and heavy weight seemed to have gone out of his bosom." Taking the same water he baptizes Marygold and she wakes, cleansed and more beautiful than ever. "Little Marygold's hair had now a golden tinge, which he had never observed in it before she had been transmuted by the effect of his kiss. This change of hue was really an improvement, and made Marygold's hair richer than in her babyhood." From then on, the epilogue reports, Midas hated the sight of gold except its glimmer in his daughter's beautiful hair. In this indirect way, Hawthorne cast the story into the form — a special affinity — and chose the images — gold, flowers, hair — which would cause the largest response. Like all heroines whose fathers have an "organic affection," Marygold is enriched by the gold of his love. Once this gold has been beaten to an airy thinness in the father, the girl is freed of his interest but rendered the more attractive as a result.[15]

Although Hawthorne adapted an old legend and an old symbolism, his colleagues devised plots which simply made the most of native currency. A daughter's virtue was equated with her father's business morality, her effect upon young men was linked to his ethics and career. In one such tale the girl goes bad when her rich father absconds. The young men "danced with her, and flirted with her, and drove her out sleighing, and took her to the theatre; but . . . went off and married someone else."[16] A corrupt father could ruin his daughter, therefore, quite as a man of probity and riches assured his daughter's success. This habit of thought is quickest demonstrated by a kind of parable, "Caught by an Heiress," in which two young girls, one beautiful and the other plain, board a Mississippi riverboat accompanied by an elderly man. Nobody can tell whose father he is or which of the girls is the heiress. Two fortune hunters, Colonel Sharp, a gambler, and Captain Deedes, an English younger son, guess that the beautiful one is the heiress and proceed to court her. Phil Pembroke, "a manly young fellow" with "a poetic reverence for a woman," agrees that she is the heiress but admires the other girl, who is merely "piquant and bright." He surprises the father and this girl in a kind of lovers' embrace and wonders if "Mr. Alexander was weak enough to think of giving his daughter a young step-mother." Of course the piquant girl is the true heiress—their embrace merely having signified their tender common regard. The putative heiress, a poor relation, had been invited to accompany them as a decoy in order that father and daughter would discover which suitors were sincere. "I have only lately become rich," the heroine explains to the manly hero who reveres women and does not lust after them; "I have not long come out of a convent, and I heard that all men were so mercenary."[17]

During the last years of the century the attachment itself and its familiar imagery, once daring, became conventional. Writers no longer tried to prove that the best women were both pure and passionate. Particularly when New Women were introduced in fiction, society realized that these independent, assertive young ladies were especially competent in love. It was not shocked, therefore, when Harold Frederic's heroine in *The Damnation of Theron Ware* turned out to be a freethinking woman of passion. Everyone expected to be told that Celia's special quality was somehow her inheritance from her father to whom she had always been "something indefinably less, indescribably more than a daughter"; that her stepmother was "a stupid, ugly, boastful old nuisance." Although it was her father's habit to "audit minutely the expenses of his household," Frederic says, he supplied Celia's separate account with "round sums." Despite a severe parsimony in other forms of love, we understand, this man gave himself without reserve to his daughter: this is the reason why she has more grace than her mother, more assurance, more vitality, and why she flourishes on an entirely new plane of feminine achievement.[18]

But it was not Frederic who, near the turn of the century, best adapted this cluster of ideas to the new manners of the time. Hamlin Garland finally organized all the traditional elements in a novel, *Rose of Dutcher's Coolly*, where he hoped to remove all the veils that hid the essential stuff of character and to inform society in matters ordinarily proscribed from popular fiction. In order to feel free to speak his mind, Garland removed the girl from her father's care and placed her in the home of a surrogate family. "I should like to adopt her, I mean, of course, take a paternal interest in her. She has appealed to me very strongly from the first . . . I'll be a father to Rose." Thus she enters the Thatchers' home. This man and his wife are childless and Rose's affection is filial as theirs is parental. At first she enjoys the role of a daughter just as Thatcher is delighted to be her father. But as she matures she begins to feel a certain impulsion of the blood which complicates her life in this home. "God knows the temptations which came to her. She had days when all the (so-called) unclean things she had ever seen, all the overheard words of men's coarse jests, came back like vultures to trouble her."

It is at this time—when she is pressed by desire—that Thatcher "came to take a different place in her love"; no longer able to frolic with him as if he "were a girl too," Rose feels that she "would never again return to that old sweet companionship with him." This troubles her fairly little, however, because she is willing to exchange Thatcher for a younger man: "she became open to the attentions of other men." Garland, it is clear, was quite as knowledgeable as Hawthorne though far less inventive or talented. As Midas provides the glister in Marygold's hair—as, indeed, countless fathers help their daughters achieve a new ripeness—so Thatcher's interest in Rose and her attachment to him help her to retain innocence yet discover sex. Within a few years Freud was to publicize this situation, so popular in our writing, and provide a clinical label. It is common knowledge, he said, that "the number of women who until late in life remain tenderly attached to father-objects is very large." Yet it is "from him, that in the normal course of development, she should find her way to her ultimate . . . choice."[19] Garland caused Rose to proceed according to plan: she feels a barrier grow between herself and Mrs. Thatcher and she decides to leave. Her "father" vows that he "will adopt no more pretty girls until I'm sixty-five." In Garland's mind he has accomplished his duty, for when Rose moves beyond adolescence she no longer requires the service of either an actual or a surrogate father. And the matter which Garland next turned her attention to is the adult problem of harmony in marriage — a New Marriage — in which she will be a "comrade and lover, not . . . subject or unwilling wife." [20]

When writers set about the task of tracing the delicate springs of the complicated American girl they turned their attention to the American domestic situation. There they discovered profound disorder and, led by the desire to report inexpungable truths, they did not hide nasty disagreements. But they preferred to stress one notable felicity, and in consequence they conceived a plot and an imagery which are as old as Western civilization. For the tale of a girl's attachment to her father is surely a familiar subject in the literature of many countries, places, times. The instance of Lot and his daughters everyone knows. Milton's portrait of the origin of sin and death is almost as famous: Satan, in incest with his daughter Sin, sires Death. Ovid's story about Myrrha and her father, Cinyras, King of Cyprus — to which Dante referred — is perhaps less well known. And it, in turn, is related to a remote Roman tale about King Antiochus who discouraged his daughter's suitors by posing a riddle — in spirit much like the riddle of the three caskets in *The Merchant of Venice*, where "the will of the living daughter," Portia says, is "curbed by the will of a dead father."

The appearance of similar situations in our writing does not, of course, imply an alarming depravity in our lives. It expresses a fantasy, not a fact; a fantasy which identifies certain longings and attitudes in society. For what occurs as incest in the early literature of civilization became, in the more sedate nineteenth century, merely an affinity which allowed genteel American novelists to say things commonly denied legitimacy or even reality. The affinity helped to explain the mystery of Woman at a time when society was troubled not only by sex but also by the feminist movement. Women who campaigned for freedom rejected traditional female duties and set about molding new aims and a new ideal. At first shocked, society later came to prefer rebellious, vigorous young women to debilitated and self-effacing girls. And it realized that New Women modeled themselves on their fathers' example, not their mothers'; that this process was rooted in the eighteenth-century effort to provide the women of the new republic with a large and beautiful opportunity to live large and dignified lives. A father who no longer taught his daughter Greek and Latin and jurisprudence nevertheless accomplished something far more precious, Americans agreed, more practical. If the best American girls harmonized passion and romance, provided the model for women everywhere—this was the work of their fathers. For these men implanted in their daughters, sometimes by accident and often by design, a sturdy sense of the honor of love. Hence all the brisk young men, reared to idolize Steel-Engraving Ladies, married Gibson Girls.

The plot, therefore, had extraordinary success. As we shall learn, Howells and James tried to say that passionate daughterhood created at least as many problems as it solved. But society at large was content, thinking that the genteel code had adapted itself to new conditions when, suddenly, Theodore Dreiser upset its aplomb. Editors who were afraid to publish *Sister Carrie* and, later, readers who were displeased by it, were distressed because the novel discarded the true system. His heroine is uncircumscribed by region, unlimited by class, and unrecognizable in origin. She is protean—an actress whose biggest success occurs when she is cast as the American Girl in Europe—and beautiful. And she is anonymous. Nobody's daughter and everybody's sister, she has no fund of paternal love to sustain or identify her yet she charms everyone. Audiences were shocked not because Carrie is a loose woman—actually she is purer than the most womanly woman because she never loses innocence—but because Dreiser had done something new in American letters. He had isolated his heroine's sexual address from the paraphernalia of society; from place, from parents, from measurable influences of any sort. Carrie violates order and stands outside degree. For Dreiser was among the first to proclaim a mode of thought which distinguishes the present from the past: desire is not so terrible as people have been taught to believe and therefore need not be defined, located, and supervised. Carrie is a foolish, pleasant, accessible girl with whom a man is on his own.[21]

♀

Nymph and nun

"The loving devotion to the father, the need to do away with the superfluous mother, and to take her place, the early display of coquetry and the arts of later womanhood, make up a particularly charming picture in a little girl and may cause us to forget . . . the grave consequences which may later result from this situation . . ."

UNLIKE Dreiser, Howells and James continued to locate a woman's unique quality in the heart of her family. Unlike Aldrich and most other writers of the day, however, they walked into the deep water and followed the stream even when it led to uncharted places — Howells because he was a very intelligent man of considerable courage and James because he was ruled by a very high discipline of art. Once the artist gets his subject, he remarked in the Preface to *The Spoils of Poynton*, there "can be for him only one truth and one direction — the quarter in which his subject most completely expresses itself." [1]

Both men decided, at about the same moment, to display the hazards of passionate daughterhood — to say that paternal influence did not invariably beautify a young woman and instead was often the source of her malaise. At first the subject interested Howells more and he wrote a series of novels — *The Rise of Silas Lapham*, *A Woman's Reason*, *A Modern Instance* — which incorporate his decisions. These are implicit in the distinction he draws between two sisters of similar breeding and talent, Irene and Penelope Lapham. Irene is pliable, dependent, innocently selfish and "babyish"; Penelope, "like her mother," is not especially "pretty but rather interesting." The hero chooses the latter and precipitates one of the main lines of action in the novel: Irene is miserable because he proposes to Penelope. When her mother tries to comfort her, she says, "icily," "Don't touch me . . . I want Papa to walk with me." She and Silas take a long walk and arrive at the large house Silas is having built in the Back Bay. This place suggests to Irene more than her father's new wealth: somehow it symbolizes Silas himself and she says "I will never live in it." Her bitterness causes her to rebel against a father whom she blames for those qualities in herself which had displeased her lover. Howells then sends her on a journey of recovery and self-discovery and when she returns she is no longer Daddy's girl. "In these few months the girl had hardened and toughened. She had lost all her babyish dependence and pliability; she was like iron." That is, she has grown into a woman—like her mother whom Silas had described as "seventy-five percent of purr-ox-eyed of *iron*."[2] Not once did Howells specifically blame Irene's situation upon her father. But one of Howells's most persistent ideas about American women—the most damning thing he said about them—is that they perpetuate girlhood long after the proper time. She is lovely, he remarked about one of his other heroines, and now has "beautiful girlhood" but after a while "the girlhood will go . . . and the girl will remain." This person, Julia Gage of *An Open-Eyed Conspiracy*, lives alone with her father and shares his spirit; he "kept her close from the other young people."[3]

It was Howells's habit, therefore, not to identify paternal influence but simply to present its effects and to interest his audience in additional, adequate reasons for the girls' failure. And if we concentrate on these we forget the first. As a result we have read *A Woman's Reason*, for example, simply as a plea for education; *A Modern Instance*, as condemnation of an immoral man and praise of divorce. Both, however, are preoccupied with girls who are ill-prepared for life and love because their fathers have trained them to be excessively filial. It was in *A Woman's Reason*, too, that he hit on an explanation which only James was to think of: the girl suffers, the father is aware of her suffering but places his joy above her sorrow. Helen Harkness and her father are "old confidantes . . . Her own mother had died long ago, and in the comradeship of her young life, her father had entered upon a second youth, happier . . . than the first." As Howells understands this situation, the father retains all the advantages. His "wife" has all the virtues of an innocent Eve. She is a docile companion whose effort is solely to please him, and he turns her into a kind of superior geisha, a dependent petted and favored but denied competence or viability. "He had that way fathers have of treating his daughter as an equal, of talking to her gravely and earnestly, and then of suddenly dropping her . . . as if she were a child." Because Helen "dutifully accepted this condition of their companionship," she remains puerile.[4] After his death her situation is perilous; she cannot remain a baby and live. Upon this problem—how can Daddy's girl learn to be independent and brave when she is prepared only for a life of dependence and timidity?—Howells built his case for a more useful education for gentlewomen.

Howells's most poignant child bride is of course Marcia Gaylord in *A Modern Instance* and he hoped to present in this woman both the charm which the alliance conferred and its cost. But he withheld from this novel his special criticism of women and placed it instead in that scene in *Lapham* where Bartley Hubbard, Marcia's unpleasant husband, interviews Silas. "I tell you," Silas says, "my wife was a *woman*."

> Bartley laughed. "That's the sort most of us marry."
>
> "No we don't," said Lapham. "Most of us marry silly little girls grown up to look like women."
>
> "Well, I guess that's so," assented Bartley . . . "I'll have to tell Marcia that."[5]

Of all Howells's heroines, Marcia is the one daughter most prettily rigged to look like a wife. This time, too, Howells did not immediately remove our attention to other matters; he located Marcia's affinity to her father deep in her heart and made it a juggernaut of the emotions. Marcia's mother left the girl's training, Howells says, almost wholly to her husband, and "in their mutual relations . . . they spoiled each other, as father and daughter are apt to do when left to themselves." Squire Gaylord did very little to discourage the trait which she shared with him and which was to provide a main reason for the failure of her marriage. "She was passionate . . . and . . . for the time being it charmed and flattered her father to have her so fond of him that she could not endure any rivalry in his affection." Gaylord's "high, hawklike profile was translated into the fine aquiline outline of hers . . . his eyes . . . had rekindled their dark fires in hers; his whole visage, softened to her sex and girlish years, looked up at him in his daughter's face."

As Marcia can endure no rivals, so the Squire resents Marcia's husband. And although Bartley is a very poor choice indeed, Howells is concerned not only with the husband's disabilities. Rather he forces us to note the effects of the Squire's "hoarded" hatred of the man who is his daughter's husband. Even Marcia is finally allowed to understand her predicament. In the courtroom when she and the Squire confront Bartley, she discovers that her father wishes not simply to see justice done but to destroy his rival. And when he demands that her husband be consigned "to a felon's cell in a felon's garb," the dutiful daughter rebels. "Marcia flung herself upon her father's arm, outstretched toward Bartley. 'No! No!' she cried . . . in a voice thick with horror. 'Never . . . I didn't understand . . . Let him go!'" Gaylord "fixed a ghastly, bewildered look upon his daughter, and fell forward across the table." [6]

Marcia's resemblance to the Squire had enhanced her style; her jealousy had signified the reserve of passion upon which her husband was to draw. But, Howells believed, no matter how charming a passionately filial girl may be, the risk is not worth the gain. Having been a favored and protected daughter, she is likely to be a petulant wife. And she brings into her marriage a father who cannot gracefully yield his prize to a stranger.

It was not Howells, however, but James who forced the subject to render the overriding ideas about character and society and love which he saw in it. *Washington Square*, like *A Modern Instance*, concerns a daughter whose life is interwoven with her father's; like Marcia, too, Catherine chooses an unsuitable lover. Both fathers resent their daughters' decision and in both instances the manifest reasons are not entirely convincing. These resemblances say that the novels share a common interest. They do not say that James chose this situation in order to represent his sense of the nature of love itself, its place in human affairs, or that he, unlike Howells, did not dissimulate and try to deny what he saw.

Both Gaylord and Dr. Sloper forbid their daughters freedom of action or of soul—the Squire by trading on Marcia's jealousy, Sloper by cutting Catherine out of his will and thus reducing her value for her fortune-hunting lover. But Marcia and her father share a tenderness. And though this eventually disables her, at first it heightened her color, braced her carriage, sharpened her inherent sensuality. Catherine is merely—and this is James's marvelously subtle effect—"good, docile, obedient and much addicted to speaking the truth" *because* Sloper has always despised her. That is to say, Sloper deprives his daughter of love and therefore reduces her charm as a woman. This physician who specializes in women's diseases tells Catherine's aunt that he knows what is best for Catherine since his interest is both paternal and professional. The aunt replies that his special competence had not saved his wife's life. Thus James did not say that Catherine's difficulties stem from her father's disregard but he allowed this fact to invade our consciousness: he built it into the logic of his story. Earlier he had written "Watch and Ward," a story based in this special affinity which reported how love can reclaim an innocent person from ruin. A young man adopts a little orphan girl whose parents are disreputable. As a result of his affection, his care, his intelligence, his scrupulousness, she grows into a lovely woman of the first order, an ideal wife. In *Washington Square*, James returned to this subject because it was the perfect occasion to detail the consequences of a denial of love.

For Sloper, unlike the man in "Watch and Ward," is incapable of love. He lost his wife and ruined his daughter. Yet he demands the prerogatives reserved only for peculiarly paternal men and thus refuses Catherine the right to live as she chooses. The clash between them occurs over Townshend's proposal of marriage. Sloper insists that he is a fortune hunter. Catherine says that she doubts it but that it does not matter—what really counts is her love for him. Sloper proves that Townshend is interested in her money—her inheritance from him. James sides with Catherine; should she receive the Sloper fortune, he says, Townshend, "an idle, amiable, selfish, and doubtless tolerably good-natured fellow," will make a pleasing enough husband. Thus James delicately introduced the issue of money as a reinforcement of his view of Catherine's deprivations. Not only is she devoid of charm because she has been deprived of her father's affection but also her attraction as a woman is negated by Sloper's refusal to make her an heiress. Left with only her meager self to offer she is bereft of all opportunity for joy. Townshend flees. She wins a final victory over her father, however, when she refuses to promise that she will not marry Townshend after Sloper dies, or to promise that she will marry at all.

I have not described all the ideas in *Washington Square* because I undertake to trace only the effects of this special affinity. James's interest was not merely in the way a father, for the very best reasons, can ruin a daughter. For he saw that this plot, which his audience would immediately recognize, could sustain his own sense of the matter: a relationship that etches character and grounds love can boomerang and become vicious.

When eleven years later, in "The Marriages," he again turned to this theme, he decided to shift the ground a little and explore the corrosive effects of a girl's intense affection for her father. Thus, by the time he came to *The Golden Bowl*, he had examined all the possibilities inherent in this affinity. In "The Marriages" James displayed the taint of distorted affection and insisted that we observe the loss of honor and love in Adela, a daughter with "fond imagination. . . . poisoned and inflamed judgment." She is her father's eldest, motherless child and she tries to wreck Papa's respectable and happy engagement to Mrs. Churchly because a new marriage, she says, will dishonor her mother's memory. She visits Mrs. Churchly and explains that her father is an impossible person who had martyred his first wife. Mrs. Churchly breaks the engagement, not, as it turns out, because she believed Adela but because she "could never live with such a girl, and as I would certainly never marry I must be sent away . . . Papa . . . refused to sacrifice me and this led . . . to their rupture. Papa gave her up . . . for me." In the final remark we face a daughter ruined for marriage but delighted by the prospect of "marriage" with her father; "Fancy the angel and fancy what I must try to be to him for the rest of his life."[7]

Adela's remark defines as well Maggie Verver's problem. For when first we meet this wonderful girl at the beginning of *The Golden Bowl*, she has recently married the great Roman Prince Amerigo but she worries lest Adam, her father, feel neglected. Her concern is not trivial: it stems from a very deep affection for her distinguished parent. A prime requirement of this novel, James recorded in his *Notebooks*, was "an intense and exceptional degree of attachment between the father and the daughter—he peculiarly paternal and she passionately filial."[8] But he was not interested in the mere privations caused by an attachment of this sort, for he designed the novel as an ornamental hymn to civilization, to the heiress herself, and therefore he reserved for it the whole weight of his choicest ideas. Indeed, this novel dramatized James's mind better than any other and epitomizes and climaxes the literature of feminine heroism in the age of gentility.

Maggie worries that her real marriage will leave Adam lonely and desperate, a prey for widows with an eye on the main chance. "It was as if . . . I kept people off, innocently, by being married to you."[9] But Adam is no mere businessman and Maggie is not simply a little girl got up like a woman. He is an equal of the great seers because he is guided by a conviction of the soul which his energy and wealth will allow him to achieve. She represents the messianic destiny of America. Their "marriage" confers upon each, therefore, a truly special distinction.

In a criticism that has become classic, F. O. Matthiessen noted that James chose for his hero a man who was unfit for the job—no mere American businessman was suited for so exacting and sophisticated a duty as James imagined for Adam. Matthiessen recalled the actual American businessman of James's day—as drawn by Charles Dana Gibson: the wizened, shrewd Yankee, intimidated by his wife, deferential to his daughter, captious and corrupt.[10] But Matthiessen disregarded the device with which James hoped to circumvent this argument. For he informs us that Adam had not always been a man with a mission but had made his fortune sailing before the stiff American breeze of opportunity; had been, we may say, at least capricious and perhaps corrupt. Indeed, his selflessness like his art collection is recent. This is explicit; but what James placed deep in the text is the process of Adam's conversion. James traced the event back to the time which immediately followed the death of Adam's wife when Maggie was ten. He and the child had come to Europe in order to forget their sorrow and though this was not a first journey, suddenly Adam, freed of his "frail, fluttering wife," had discovered with "a mute inward gasp" that "to rifle the Golden Isles" was "the business of his future." And this discovery made him "equal somehow with the great seers." He is a new man: "He had been nothing of the kind before—too decidedly . . . not." But now, alone with his child, he understands that his wife had been indefinably the reason for his failure. Indeed, actual marriage itself was a reason why Europe had not led him to his vision "on that earlier occasion, the journey of his honeymoon year"; then the revelation of his high duty "had still been closely covered."[11]

James introduced these ideas while Adam reflects on his past. And, he wonders, if his wife were still alive, would she have "prevented him from ever scaling his vertiginous peak—or would she . . . have been able to accompany him to that eminence." Because "no companion of Cortez had presumably been a real lady," Adam decides against his wife. But not against Maggie. She is her mother, he says, and something more; she is a real lady, that is, and something else. Thus James injected, so delicately that we nearly miss its place, Maggie's role in Adam's conversion. Although James's vision is high, his idea grandiose, and his mood sublime, his subject is usual. He turned a metaphorical marriage into an alliance of the spirit. And a passionately filial daughter of the usual sort is turned into a woman who can stir the imagination of a seer, steer him to an "exemplary passion for perfection," and help him to decide to propagate a religion, to envision "civilization condensed, concrete, consummate, set down by his hands as a house on a rock."[12] Adam's conversion is ineffable but in substance it duplicates, in Howells's novel, Harkness's new and larger joy in his life with

Helen. Like most fathers in genteel American novels, Adam is happier with his daughter than he had been with his wife. But James turned this fact into a subtle mystic conversion to an ideal of duty which no mere husband can know. Incidentally, the allegory which Quentin Anderson suggests is enlarged by our understanding of Maggie's role in Adam's mind: love embodied in Maggie causes the reform and conversion of the old, inept Adam and helps him to establish the New Jerusalem.

In the vocabulary of the novel Maggie is "a creature of . . . the cinquecento at its most golden hour"; her innocence and radiance were of "the colour—of what on earth? Of what but the extraordinary American good faith . . . and yet at the same time of her imagination."[13] She is truly fortune's darling. But when the novel opens, Maggie has absolutely no perception of her duty and no understanding of her effect upon her father. She knows only that she loves this distinguished man and fears that her marriage will make him suffer. She is not aware that Adam's reliance upon her has given him all the advantages; brought joy and self-fulfillment because through her he learned how to realize himself. For him, however, "marriage" has done its work and is no longer useful. He is delighted by Amerigo because now his daughter can fulfill her part of their unconscious, tacit contract. Adam will strip America of naiveté by exhibiting there the relics of the saints of the Old World; Maggie will reform evil old Europe. As Maggie inspires her father, so Adam trains his daughter for her own crucial work. She is both a doting child, conventionally timid and dependent, and later, when she truly becomes Amerigo's wife, a woman of destiny. Their marriage is a vision of that new order intimated in *The Portrait of a Lady*, ineffable in *The Wings of the Dove*. But *The Golden Bowl* integrates the tender affinity and the international situation in order to define Maggie's special fitness for the job James created for the very best conceivable American woman. Retaining her goodness, Maggie will reform her husband, in whose past there are "archives, annals, infamies"—"a wicked pope." Amerigo welcomes her virtue, admires it, and contracts this marriage because he desires "some new history that should contradict, and even . . . flatly dis-

honor, the old."[14] Maggie's influence, unlike Milly Theale's, is not to await her death. Endowing the Prince with her father's millions — and with the riches of her person gained through "marriage" to Adam — then acquiring from her real husband a sense of history, she will fulfill the whole obligation of the quintessential American girl: Maggie and Amerigo will reform the world. Fortune's darling can do her work, James says, only when she truly loves her husband and achieves in him an effect similar to that she had provoked in her father.

The whole second half of the novel, then, relates how poor little Maggie comes to shrive herself of Adam. Like Marcia Gaylord, she has never learned how to be a proper wife. As Ibsen said of Hedda Gabler, she must "be regarded rather as her father's daughter than as her husband's wife." Having received from Adam her education in greatness, Maggie cannot at first give up their intimacy and her reliance upon him; her husband is merely another object for Adam's collection. James chose a number of ways to say this and it is notable that he used a variant of Howells's sense that these girls have only the dress and manners of women. "She dresses . . . as much for her father — and always did — as for herself. She has her room in his house very much as she had it before she was married."[15] Her child, too, is converted into "a link between a mamma and a grandpa";[16] and though James intended this as an irony it represents his understanding of the forces which bound Maggie to Adam at the very moment when, as Joyce was very soon to remark, the new Viennese school was occupied with precisely these matters. Indeed, he knew very well what he was about for later he dropped the irony and instead sympathized with her: Verver was "deep in her heart and in her life; too deep down, as it were, to be disengaged, contrasted or opposed, in short objectively presented."[17] This was of course Aaron's effect on Theodosia and I think we can take James's analysis as an adequate view of the common neurosis. For Maggie's engagement forces her to prefer insulation to experience, dependence to autonomy, and therefore deprives her of real immersion in real marriage: she cannot fulfill her destiny because she prefers perpetual girlhood. "Do you realize, father," she says, "that I've never had the least blow?" She knows nothing, Maggie admits, about wounds and shames—"I don't *want* to know!"[18] Because she is "the creature in the world to whom a wrong thing could least be communicated" she must learn "what's called Evil—with a very big E" and it must be disagreeable enough "to make her sit up . . . to make her decide to live."[19]

The evil to which Maggie must be initiated is both the adultery which she has forced Amerigo and Charlotte into and the price in dignity and honor which her innocence costs. Her father no longer needs her: have you felt forsaken? Charlotte had asked Adam in answer to his proposal of marriage. Is there room in his life, she wonders, "for another daughter"? Adam had replied "fiercely"; must a man be all his life nothing "but a father"?[20] No, he had answered, he had *not* felt forsaken. Later Maggie understands this and the moment when understanding occurs, as we shall see, is itself beautiful. But the chief sign of Maggie's understanding, of her decision to live, is contained in the destruction of the golden bowl itself, James's complicated symbol of the complex action of his long novel. The bowl, gilt over cracked glass, refers to adultery, Amerigo, Maggie's imperfect marriage, Europe. And when Maggie decides for "a happiness without a hole in it," she decides to disengage herself from the intimacy with Adam, and allows Mrs. Assingham to smash the bowl. Among many intimations, then, passionate daughterhood itself is embodied in the bowl. Its flaw evokes Maggie's degrading attachment, the gilt that covers the crack is exactly as meretricious as Maggie's golden innocence. As the bowl was once precious but, cracked, is valueless, so the Ververs' affinity was once beautiful—inspired Adam, distinguished Maggie—but is now evil.

Maggie has great imagination, however, and foregoing this bowl, sets out to shape another, one that will hold "all our happiness in it"—Amerigo's and hers. And she accomplishes this first by getting Adam to agree that he and his new wife, Charlotte, will leave for America. The museum must be established. But she has the harder job of expunging Adam from the tissues of her heart, of freeing herself to assume the duties imposed by her dynastic marriage. James wrote this event into that wonderful scene where Charlotte is playing the role of cicerone in Adam's English house, a duty which foreshadows her lifelong occupation in America. It is on this occasion that Maggie discovers how Verver had used her, had required her and therefore had so long doomed her, had deprived her of personality, of honor, of that sexual competence, even, which as Amerigo's wife she must have. The moment is sudden but it presents James's sense that Verver uses his women to fulfill his sublime needs. Placed at opposite ends of the gallery, Maggie and Adam overhear Charlotte's lecture and suddenly Maggie feels "the strangest thing to be happening." Charlotte's voice sounded "like the shriek of a soul in pain" and Maggie felt "herself turn with a start to her father."

> "Can't she be stopped? Hasn't she done it enough?"—some such question . . . she let herself ask him to suppose in her. Then it was that, across half the gallery . . . he struck her as confessing with strange tears in his eyes, to sharp identity of emotion. "Poor thing, poor thing."

The moment holds the rationale of the entire fiction. Maggie thinks she and her father share a common sympathy for Charlotte; then James explodes the fantasy. As Maggie stares at Adam wondering why he forces Charlotte's soul to shriek, thinking that he agrees it must end, "held thus together they had still another strained minute." Then "the shame, the pity, the better knowledge, the smothered protest, the divined anguish even, so overcame him that, blushing to his eyes, he turned short away." When Adam sees that Maggie for the first time has discovered her own sacrifice to him, sees her anguish in discovery, he blushes and turns away. Maggie finally knows that the "marriage" with her father had not been an innocent idyll. And after the first moment of horror, knowledge exhilarates, excites her. "The affair was but of a few muffled moments, this snatched communion yet lifted Maggie as on air—so much for deep guesses on her own side it gave her to think of." Now she feels foolish. "And it wasn't closed to her . . . that the deepest depth of all . . . was that you couldn't know for sure some of your own compunctions and contortions wouldn't show for ridiculous."[21] Freed, her mind immediately turns to Amerigo:

Adam is exorcised. James explains Adam's motive, saying that "he may be sublime, sublimer even than Maggie herself." [22] And when finally Maggie says farewell she is no longer a child but the heroic daughter of a sublime father. Like Theodosia Burr, she is proud to be this man's daughter. But their final embrace dramatizes a new kind of affection between a great man and a magnificent woman. "He held her hard and kept her long, and she let herself go; but it was an embrace that, august and almost stern, produced for all its intimacy no revulsion and broke into no inconsequence of tears." [23] The embrace produced no revulsion because it is no longer degrading, and no tears because each knows the other is fated to fulfill the highest hopes of history. Thus James wove into an allegory—Mr. Anderson's account of the effect on James of his father's religious system may show in the novel still another dimension—the stuff of culture and of personality. Taking the familiar plot and recognizing in it what psychoanalysts call the female oedipal situation, James imposed an especially personal order. It does full justice to his view of human aspiration and dignity and, coincidentally, presents as cogent a description as has yet been devised of the ways character is formed.

Nearly the last words of the novel are Amerigo's to Maggie, kept for the instant after the Ververs have left. "I see nothing but *you*," he says. *You* is America in all its goodness and imagination. But the word is inseminated with the sexual moment too. Maggie's awakening to Evil has been accompanied by an awakening to the sweet sexuality of her husband. But until she was free of Adam she was unable to respond. Now she is ready to be the responsive lover of the man whom her love is to guide, to whom her money will provide the power for reform. The Prince's remark is in effect a sexual invitation and now she is able, joyfully, to respond. The rebellion, the victory, and the moment are complete. We may say, too, that a whole cycle of literature has been completed. For when Maggie turns to her husband, she behaves in the precise fashion Hawthorne had imagined as best suited to an "angel and apostle of the coming revelation," the "destined prophetess" of the new truth of love which, so Hester Prynne believed, would establish "the whole relation of man and woman on a surer ground of mutual happiness."

The Golden Bowl is James's most exacting, skillful, and ambitious novel chiefly because it intertwines his perception of the complexity of love with his vision of the future of civilization. And he based its future in its application of certain human qualities which he believed were rooted in America and others which he traced to Europe. Innocence, good faith, honor, energy, freedom were the terms in his mind when he recalled a society that had declared its independence from a history of human debasement. Continuity, order, pageantry, deep understanding of human degradation were forces that molded the European imagination. Join the two sensibilities, American and European, and you create a new morality and a truly new world. As we know, James and his generation agreed that the American girl best symbolized the first; for the second, any proper European prince would do. James's colleagues were content to compose entertainments based on these ideas but James saw himself as an equal of the seers because these ideas composed the religion he wished to propagate. His final act of desperation, of misery, his assuming British citizenship, came about because he felt betrayed. America should have seen its divine duty, immediately entered the War, and saved the world from the Hun—from precisely the kind of infamy this society was designed to counteract.[24]

The act was desperate, however, because it denied his own understanding of the matter: harmony of the self must precede harmony and dedication in society. His whole career expresses this Socratic vision: before an American woman can achieve her destiny—to reorder the world through the effect of Love—she must herself learn the meaning of love. Like Verena Tarrant, she must grow conscious of the power of sex and refuse to debase or sentimentalize this power. She can acquire understanding only when she reconciles the northness of her nature with its southness, eastness with westness, chastity with magnetism. Unlike Daisy Miller or Isabel Archer, she may not remain provincial and inept in its management. And she must not allow herself to be robbed, like Catherine Sloper, of sexual competence, of the capacity for love. The source of this capacity, James said, is a necessary degree of passionate daughterhood. Just how much was required to distinguish a woman, and what amount rendered a woman infantile and disordered, he was not able to say. He realized that the matter was slippery and yet crucial, dangerous yet not irredeemable. Sex, James agreed with Maupassant, was the moral antecedent to love. And love is the hope and distinction of man. Thus Maggie Verver, who combined the qualities of a nymph and a nun, finally reconciled all antitheses; she fulfilled the American dream of love, the dream of all the ages.

♀

Sugar and spice

"To the woman of the period . . . restless, seductive, greedy, discontented, craving sensation, unrestrained, a little selfish, intelligent, uneducated, sybaritic, following blind instincts and perverse fancies, slack of mind as she is trim of body, neurotic and vigorous . . . fit mate for the hurried, reckless and cynical man of the age, predestined mother of—what manner of being?: To Her I dedicate [*Flaming Youth*]."

MAGGIE VERVER, in her own right, is one of the most beautiful women in literature. Her astonishing brilliance, Philip Rahv observed, exhibits James's "progressively rising estimate of that American fate" which the greater part of his work describes. "The account opens with the simple, almost humble instances of Mary Garland and Daisy Miller, who are baffled and shamed by Europe," and closes with the "prodigious success of Maggie Verver, to whom Europe offers itself as a dazzling, and inexhaustible opportunity." [1] Inexhaustible, we must add, because she is more resourceful than any of James's other heroines: she alone is free to enrich herself and civilization.

But she represents, too, a society that was dissolving at the moment when James organized its commodities and values in one golden novel. We are accustomed to date the twentieth century from 1914. This date marks at least the figurative demise, we say, of Victorianism in Edwardian England, a powerful social aristocracy in France, gentility in America. In 1905 Lily Bart in Mrs. Wharton's *The House of Mirth* is ruined because, unchaperoned, she had spent an hour in a man's rooms. But in 1914, in Sinclair Lewis's first novel, *Our Mister Wrenn*, the heroine's charm is increased because she takes a walking trip through Europe alone with a man. No longer merely a New Woman, she is a New Intellectual who reads Nietzsche and Shaw, drinks in public, goes uncorseted, talks about sex. Unlike Maggie and Lily, who precede her by only a decade, she is a modern girl. But when the genteel tradition was overthrown what replaced it was not, as the new writers planned, a solid acceptance of love and life.

Istra's appearance in Lewis's novel, however, was heralded with astounding suddenness by the new sounds played on the fiddles that John Butler Yeats said were tuning all over America. Between 1910 and 1920, insurgent intellectuals and rebels took over control of culture and literature from Paul Elmer More, Irving Babbitt, William Crary Brownell. Disgust with conservative capitalist economics created a new labor journal, *Masses*, edited by Max Eastman and John Reed. Revulsion against polite verse created *Poetry*, whose foreign editor was Ezra Pound; against polite fiction, led to the formation of Mabel Dodge Luhan's literary salon in Greenwich Village and, later, Van Wyck Brooks's proclamation of a new hope for American literature, *America's Coming-of-Age*. Impatience with Brander Matthews's idea of a theater established the Provincetown Players, Eugene O'Neill, and eventually the Theatre Guild. After 1920, Mencken and his friends, James Branch Cabell and Carl Van Vechten, lambasted or mocked American provincialism in religion and morals. And by 1925 the manners and opinions of the age of gentility seemed antediluvian to Lewis and Sherwood Anderson, Hemingway and Fitzgerald. These men refused to be, as Lewis later said in his Nobel Prize speech — in which he referred by name to Hemingway, Thomas Wolfe, Thornton Wilder, Michael Gold, Dos Passos, Faulkner — "genteel and traditional and dull." Their job was to achieve a great victory over the forces of vested prudery and massed property.

Despite Lewis's brave words, nobody was very happy. Society celebrated "the 'new' freedom, the 'new' morality," and the arts reported "the new disillusion." [2] By 1915, indeed, the seeds of disillusion had taken root and sufficient numbers of the rich had automobiles in which casual dalliance by young people became comparatively free-wheeling. And the boys reported their success and their sadness in the *Yale Record* or *Princeton Tiger*. By 1920, through a kind of sexual Republicanism which said that what was good for the very rich was good for the country, children everywhere acted inflamed. People seemed to want to assure one another that they had shed naiveté. Everybody attributed these changes to the War, to pentup energies which the War released. The young men who rushed to serve in the ambulance corps or the new air corps discovered that they, like Lieutenant Henry in *A Farewell to Arms*, were "made to . . . eat and drink and sleep with Catherine." But release was momentary: Hemingway and Fitzgerald, Dos Passos, even Faulkner came to believe that the War killed everything—particularly love. As a result they stopped believing in love and agreed with D. H. Lawrence and Mabel Dodge Luhan: everyone must believe in passion. What had been initiated by Dreiser, Lewis, and Anderson, therefore, as a revolt against the genteel conspiracy, the War dramatized and fulfilled. From a "sexless angel in the skies" to "a most sexy flapper"—this descent was called the Fall of Woman.[3] Finally the writers of the Lost Generation succeeded in doing what such diverse men as Garland and James had urged: they stripped idealism from passion.

This was an act of will and it caused very striking discomfort; indeed, it underlies their acceptance of Gertrude Stein's opinion that they were lost. They did not realize that almost exactly because they rejected the genteel vision of love they felt bereft. Both Hemingway and Fitzgerald, for example, despised the hypocrisies and repudiated the warnings of gentility but they were men bred and sustained by its religion of love. They thought that their leaders were O'Neill or Sherwood Anderson: in 1937 Thomas Wolfe wrote to Fitzgerald saying that he and Hamilton Basso had arranged a joint pilgrimage to Anderson. Earlier O'Neill had written *Diff'rent* which, aided by the psychoanalytic gossip of the day, announced that a fine girl is turned into a virago when the ideal of chastity repressed the natural forces. Feeling that society could not be reordered except through a kind of nihilism, they closed their minds to history. They learned little from Howe or Eggleston, Mrs. Wharton or James, who had insisted—as blandly but as intently as they could—that when sex is demeaned, capricious or disabled women result. Had Anderson or Hemingway or Fitzgerald understood the meaning of the past, they would not have felt heroic or bereft nor would they have created a religion of sex which did not please them or convince their audience. For by 1926, Fitzgerald said, "The universal preoccupation with sex had become a nuisance." "There are all kinds of love in the world," he mourned in *All the Sad Young Men*, "but never the same love twice." Gloria Gilbert, "the most celebrated and sought-after young beauty in the country," seemed "sort of . . . unclean."[4] Hemingway, as Edmund Wilson has remarked, never succeeded "in making love a two-way enterprise; the women are silently submissive instruments not autonomous personalities." And when Hemingway decided to portray a man in whom the capacity for devotion is coherent and compelling he chose Jake Barnes and made him impotent. Then he offered Lady Brett to Jake — that promiscuous, disorganized, noble woman. Their love was ideal: it wed a modern woman of passion to the soul of an emasculated man.

The achievement of these men and those that preceded them prepared the way for the writers who have become prominent since the Second War. The latest literary generation came to maturity in an occasion different indeed from that of the twenties and thirties. Old taboos were destroyed and new subjects forced into literature. A new audience — the new middle classes — had been created among large numbers of fairly well-educated people. It is, too, an audience trained by twentieth-century literature to expect that its emotions and its intimacies will be treated without affectation and with verve. But modern writing has not fulfilled its obligations to its past or elaborated the vision of love which this tradition in American writing composed. The Ohio Females foolishly made idealization of Woman the first duty of men and the first requisite of love. The fictions of our era — the posturing of Cabell and Van Vechten, Anderson's mysticism, the turgid muscularity and frantic bed-hopping of the twenties and thirties, the sexual greed, perversion, and hyperbole of the forties — have done scarcely more than adapt the old mystique to our confused taste. Twentieth-century fiction has not fitted sex into a coherent scheme of love or created a climate of understanding so intelligent or comprehensive as that inspired by gentility. "Like palm reading with Pilar," John W. Aldridge says of *For Whom the Bell Tolls*, "sex with Maria was an entrance into the unknown. In the frenzy of intercourse, the earth moved. Sex even had something to do with Jordan's political convictions." [5] But this is very fuzzy. And Hemingway, his predecessors and his imitators, the naturalists of his generation as well as the symbolists of the latest generation, discover in sex a mere drug, a momentary relief from the burden of war or the torture of self-confrontation in peace.

Having rejected the public symbols of gentility, our writers have not yet rediscovered its private and distinguished understanding of the connections among idealism, sex, love, and civilization — the supreme achievement of the genteel tradition. And there are no women as beautiful as Maggie. Indeed, in contemporary fiction women are scarcely people at all but counters in a game of sex. When women are feminine and are not masculinized, they are mere objects lusted after and lusty, in the manner of Nathanael West's *The Day of the Locust* or Christopher Isherwood's more recent *The World in the Evening*. These are novels about Hollywood, its bristling desires and amateurish vices, which somehow evoke the newest in a long line of Sister Carries, Marilyn Monroe. Although these writers degrade sex they realize that it cannot, as Merle Miller or Frederick Wakeman thinks it can, replace motive or substitute itself for people. For one of their most popular feminine types is, absurdly, the suburban medusa in whose eye men somehow discover a certain primitive, terrifying carnality. The most awesome person at the country club, says a writer for the *Ladies' Home Journal*, is the woman whose manner implies a question, "Well, big boy, what are you going to do about me?" [6] Men quiver and prefer her counterpart, a motherly or a sisterly woman of the sort presented by Tennessee Williams or Gore Vidal. And there are the grotesque women — either mountainous or miniscule — of Carson McCullers, to whom love is a bondage of the spirit which distorts the flesh, at once the source of hope and the exact condition of frustration. Indeed, if we except the heroines of Robert Penn Warren and Saul Bellow, the most charming girl seems to be a "career girl with the uncontrollable passion for taking strange young men into her bed." [7] That she will make the happiest of marriages and the best of wives is what the left hand writes, while the right hand says that once married she is awesome or sisterly or unfaithful. Very few of our writers—Wright Morris is another exception—seem to realize that long ago they were presented a grammar, rhetoric, and vocabulary of sex; that "sex has certain manifestations which are socially quite complex, that it is involved with religion, politics and the fate of nations," and is occasionally marked "by a liveliness of energy which sometimes glows to incandescence." [8] In our day the moral imagination has not been enriched by the sexual imagination and instead the sexual imagination has been depleted.

When the American dream thus lost its cogency, its central values—love, sex, and freedom—no longer blended to form an image of the world. Furthermore, our writers simply disregarded the tradition that underlies the appearance of each heroine in our literature. Now love is identified with sex and conceived as something special—not sacred, merely apart from the main business of life—very hard to get, a gift that the lover takes because he has been trained by what David Riesman calls the only scheme of values in America today: the values and virtues of consumption. "I'll buy that" has replaced "I want to know." In part because serious literature rejects this morality, it imagines each act or decision—in sex, politics, war—as an event in itself. And what Riesman names other-directedness is accompanied by fragmentation. *Togetherness* is a game of let's pretend that we know why we live and what we live for. Until recently, Faulkner was the only novelist to organize all the traditional elements in a single moral vision. But his best opinion of love—illustrated by Lena in *Light in August*—is that it is motivated by an impulse to maternality. And this is not an adequate view of its complexity or power.

In illustration of the contemporary mode, I have chosen two leading themes in literature and popular culture. The first concerns the heroine who, in the age of gentility, unified goodness and badness. Disclosing her place in the contemporary imagination, tracing her sources, we discover that now she is isolated from other women; her unique charm has been adapted to values conceived on Madison Avenue. In 1950, a study of heroines in American, French, and British films described the kinds of women each culture seems to admire most. The usual French heroine is a bad woman and where a conflict arises between a good and a bad girl, the man usually prefers the bad. The British heroine does not fit either category, but is rather a fine woman loved by both good and bad men. The good man is satisfied with her as she is, and the bad man degrades her and does not yield to "her ennobling influence as he is apt to do in American films." The American girl alone combines "the exciting qualities of the bad girl and the comradely loyalty of the good one — in one prize package." She seems promiscuous, but "sexual wickedness has . . . become a mere external ornament, a forepleasure stimulous to wholesome love."[9] The editors of *Time*, two years earlier, had been more succinct: "to millions of Americans, the pert, sexy but basically 'nice' American girl that Betty [Grable] plays on the screen is young American womanhood at its best."[10]

This person, obviously, embodies the commonest current opinion of love. It is an opinion that stems from the genteel tradition. In an earlier time it was represented by a union of North and South, magnetism and prudery, nymph and nun, East and West. As a matter of fact, the heroine of modern films has a discernible genealogy which returns us to the place where the reconciliation was most dramatic, the American heartland. Miss Grable — as well as more recent equally popular actresses — inherited her place from such women as Claudette Colbert and Katharine Hepburn or Carole Lombard who, in the thirties, established this dualism through a kind of masculinization of feminine character. During the depression, these women played poor little rich girls who rebelled against their class, their fathers, almost against their sex. They proved that women were men's equals in deviltry and violence. Their films concern a man and woman "who hit each other, throw each other down, mock each other, play with each other."[11] It was Tocqueville who remarked that American women are feminine but have the hearts and minds of men. In a group of films of which *It Happened*

One Night is the most famous, women demonstrated that they had similar sexual energy too.

At that time people began to wonder what had happened to "the old-fashioned vamp." Where was Theda Bara? Not only had her popularity waned but also the "innocent lady" had lost caste. "Both seem . . . to be replaced by our modern leading lady" who combined "sweetness and charm" with "loose morals." [12] Earlier, this arrangement had created Clara Bow's effect too and she had portrayed the kind of person Lewis, Van Vechten, and Fitzgerald had chosen for fiction. Like Istra Nash, she was "athletic, hoydenish," an "almost sexless figure about whom conversations about sex continually raged." [13] Even this device, incidentally, was exhumed for the recent film, *The Moon Is Blue*: the man asks the girl why she seems to talk only about sex and she answers, "Don't you think it's better for a girl to be preoccupied with sex than occupied?"

The translation of this heroine from fiction to films occurred sometime after the end of the First World War. Van Vechten, for example, wrote *Spider-Boy* in 1924 about a wealthy girl who wants to be an actress in films. This was clairvoyant and daring: Wilhemina Ford is simply a more candid Gibson Girl. "I'm always proposing to you," she tells the hero, "You're the only man I've ever considered marrying." Her morals are unimpeachable but her manners would have shocked the New Woman of the nineties. Indeed, the revolution itself—its minor changes of and its essential unity with the past—is palpable in the scene where the girl's father holds a pistol to the hero's head. He is attempting to force the young man into marriage when Wilhemina walks into the room and asks her father what he thinks he is doing. With royal manliness he says that he will save her "from this fiend."

"Didn't he abduct you from your home and try to seduce you?" he demanded.

"If there's been any seduction going on it's been on my part. I left home to go into the movies and I met Ambrose on the train . . . I told him immediately that I might marry him and I've been telling him ever since." [14]

She is simply a film-struck Western girl to whom sex is neither divine nor mordant and she feels no shame for a healthy desire. The Rousseauistic mode of the nineteenth century—when Western savages were naturally noble and therefore could be tamed—was simplified and domesticated.

But it was not Wilhemina alone who established the good-bad girl's pre-eminence in American fiction and films, for there is one final link that helps to establish Miss Grable's genealogy. Also it returns to the heartland itself, where, in the eighties, the embrace between the good woman and the bad had established the most suitable symbol of personal and national harmony. This was the most convincing in a history of similar methods—Poe's, Hawthorne's, James's, Moody's; the half-sisters of the nineties, the frigid white goddesses and the nubile slaves of the 1920's—because society believed that Western girls were the most authentically American. When in 1912, therefore, Booth Tarkington wrote *The Flirt*, he portrayed an Indiana which even then was mythic, no longer raw or savage but instead bucolic. As the region was now serene, so the Middle Western character was integrated rather than dissociated, a coherent, rounded product of its past: "Hoosier" no longer referred to the wild Kentuckian, merely to a native Indianan of whatever origin. Thus the hero of this novel, a businessman of honor, reminds the heroine of "a handsome young circuit rider" such as her grandmother had once described. He belongs, the girl thinks, "in those old, old times." He is not a religionist; but he is the grandson, in virtue and energy, of the Methodist circuit rider. And the two women, Cora and Laura, are the granddaughters in spirit of Eggleston's Nancy and Roxy. Now, however, they are sisters, bred to the same traditions and pervaded with the same inheritance. What has been lost is a sense of fear: Nancy was dangerous, subdued after a brutal struggle. But Cora is merely a flirt. She is a fatal woman indeed—she drives a man to drink—but she maintains the pose of innocence. A "precocious huntress," a "Carmen," she wears a "white flaming crescent in her hair" which inflames her Southern lover, a man heated by region and drink, who "had an almost perfect understanding of a part of her nature."[15] In this fashion Tarkington introduced the qualities of the bad woman alongside those of the good, and created one heroine whose frontier badness was harmonized with her civilized goodness. Tarkington simply substituted new savageries for old: Cora marries a shrewd man with money, one destined to be a captain of industry. And a few years later she displayed herself in a silent film called *Bad Sister*.

By the twentieth century, therefore, savagery was forgotten or incorporated into a symbiosis of love and conceived as mere flirtatiousness. In our day it reappears as a reassurance of sexual ability, an overture to wholesome love. "What is the American girl made of?" asks a manufacturer of cosmetics in the *New York Times*. "Sugar and spice and everything nice?" His reply accomplishes two things: it expresses the belief that something new has happened to American women. And it dramatizes that search for unity which this theme represents and which so long ago was established in our souls.

Not since the days of the Gibson girl! There's a *new* American beauty . . . she's tease and temptress, siren and Gamin, dynamic and demure. Men find her slightly and delightfully baffling. Sometimes a little maddening. Yet they admit she's *easily* the most exciting woman in the world. She's the 1952 American beauty with a fool-proof formula for melting a male! She's the "Fire and Ice" girl. (Are *you*?)[16]

There is, then, an almost straight line connecting Tarkington's Cora and the Fire and Ice Girl. She expresses our sensibility quite as the Steel-Engraving Lady and the Gibson Girl expressed the genteel sensibility. During more than a hundred years, if we trust the testimony of our literature, society has attempted to blend two opposing opinions of love. And in our day it appears readier than at any time in its past to balance both. In the past, however, literature tried to penetrate the realities that underlay disunity, and eventually it found its way to a symbol that dramatized its discoveries. Today, the symbol which once expressed the highest achievement of the New World has become a huckster's toy.

When we turn to the second theme, the special affinity linking fathers and daughters, we discover that it no longer provides a schematic comprehension of freedom and love.[17] Instead daughterhood is treated tenuously, frivolously, or psychiatrically. American writers seem to agree that one of the most interesting subjects is the process through which a woman discovers herself. But today her life has no special texture because it is composed of more or less related elements among which, invariably, is the undefined but pervasive spirit of her father: except for Robert Penn Warren's novel, *Band of Angels*, freedom, love, and Daddy are in separate compartments.

The international heroine, for example, formerly an heiress who was somehow enriched by her father, today no longer requires even that vague identification. She exists in her own right, a somewhat finished product of a moderately cohesive group of states. She has become a familiar person in musical comedy where her bounce, her spontaneity, her wit, her impatience with red tape or protocol, her friendliness and self-assurance continue to be her most notable qualities. And she continues to evoke the kind of lapidary comment so usual in the last century: Stephen Spender has replaced Paul Bourget. "Certain American women recall portraits by Titian or Rubens—as do certain European ones—but whereas the Europeans are like remote descendants of the models for those paintings, the Americans have the freshness and newness of some dusty portrait from which the varnish has been removed, revealing the colours of the glowing flesh in their almost shocking brilliance." Their beauty reconciles "the classicism of the Renaissance with the freedom of the New World"—and is a "very American" beauty indeed.[18] An observation of this sort is, to my mind, factitious, a little dishonest. It is so self-conscious that you cannot feel the emotion which it is intended to evoke and instead must substitute wonder at the sentience of its author. Then you wonder if there was any emotion to speak of.

This girl is no longer naive or unequipped for love, however, and she is ready to go to bed with the right man—plantation owner, prince, or prime minister. Indeed, sometimes she is accused of being merely avid rather than vital. That is to say, she has a kind of animal greed and violence. No longer is this quality traced, as

Mrs. Wharton believed Undine Spragg's avidity could be traced, to her father's lawlessness. The girl long ago received her inheritance, literature implies, and if she uses it now in an effort to buy joy—her prototype is Barbara Hutton—the decision is hers. Geoffrey Gorer, incidentally, has remarked this turnabout on the nineteenth-century legend of French lubricity, its replacement with a corresponding legend about American women. This legend is notable in the film *An American in Paris*, where the rich American playgirl invites the artist-hero to her rooms and says that she will sponsor him. It is clear, however, that what she wants is the man and he flees, scared by her unfeminine boldness. He prefers a demure French virgin. But if the huntress frightens native Americans, she seems to suit a current European notion about this country. Her violence embodies what the French existentialist novelists—Sartre, Simone de Beauvoir—like to imagine is peculiarly American: an unrestrained acceptance of the human condition.[19] It is striking, too, that a much younger French writer, Mlle. Sagan, wrote a very popular novel, *Bonjour Tristesse*, which is unique in French letters in that it turns to the source of American feminine assertiveness, passionate daughterhood.

The American heroine is no longer incisively herself. The quality of a girl's love continues to define her nature and this in turn is still linked to her father's quality. But literature, like society, pretends she is on her own. This pretense alternates, too, with the kind of innocence that creates foolish dramas on television. Only one is worth mentioning, *My Little Margie*, a weekly series that played from June 1952, until August 1955. "The plot has curious Freudian undertones," one reviewer remarked; a father and daughter do nothing more than try "to keep each other from falling in love with outsiders who might break up their cozy family of two." This drama achieved the distinction of being the first "radio and TV show to span three networks" despite the fact that it was disliked by critics and was expected to vanish "after a brief stint as a summer replacement."[20] Its popularity attests its relevance in an audience which sought reprints of a pamphlet prepared for the New England Mutual Life Insurance Company, called *What Is a Girl?* "God borrows from many creatures to make a little girl. He uses the song of a bird, the squeal of a pig, the stubbornness of a mule, the antics of a monkey, the spryness of a grasshopper, the curiosity of a cat, the speed of a gazelle, the slyness of a fox, the softness of a kitten, and to top it all off He adds the mysterious mind of a woman." Despite the bother that she causes, the author concludes, "she can make you a king when she climbs on your knee and whispers, 'I love you best of all!' "[21]

I love you best of all, of course, is about what Theodosia Burr said to her father, echoed by countless disabled women in the last century. But frivolity, tenuousness, and a disregard of history today are the more striking in that Fitzgerald years ago wrote *Tender Is the Night*. Based on a psychiatric understanding of love, it is a deadly serious story which is continuous with the tradition. Arthur Mizener says that Fitzgerald thought he was "shooting at something like *Vanity Fair*."[22] But his novel relies on uniquely American plots, inherited not only from *The Golden Bowl* but also from a procession of stories in the ladies' magazines. Fitzgerald wanted to show the genesis of beauty and ripeness in love as well as the source of horror and infertility. For the first, a display of the best way for love to occur in the gentle heart, he chose Rosemary Hoyt and provided her with the most suitable biography he could conceive. She is the only child of a widowed mother. Unlike poor widows of earlier generations who guard their daughters against bestial men, Mrs. Hoyt is a woman of sensibility. She realizes that Rosemary is excessively dependent. She realizes, too, that a woman must not be prim. And Fitzgerald, wishing to protect Rosemary's innocence but also to intimate her availability, chose a remarkable method of combining the two. She is an actress, he said, whose first real success is in a film called "Daddy's Girl": thus he implied that she is pure but accessible—she has no real father, merely his shadow. And her mother urges her to "sever the umbilical cord" by finding a real man who can introduce her to the process of love. Dick Diver performs this service and Rosemary discovers true splendor. The end of their affair, like the end of Maggie's with Adam, causes no inconsequence of tears because it has provided her with a stern sense of the dignity of love. Some day, she says, "I'm going to find somebody and love him and love him and never let go." Unconfused and undismayed by an attachment to a real father Rosemary moves without pain from adolescence to womanhood, from dependence to devotion.

Nicole Warren, however, was literally Daddy's girl. Incest was the consequence of affinity, and childishness, dependence, and a destructive illness were the results of incest. What is merely a fantasy in earlier literature, an intuition, a generalized malaise, Fitzgerald made specific and real. Doubtless he used ideas picked up during his long connection with psychiatry, but his prehensile imagination turned whatever it was that he learned into coherent and, during most of the novel, powerful fiction. Nicole was eleven —perhaps thirteen: he contradicts himself but he wants to say that she had come to an age of puberty—when her mother died and her father became "father and mother both to her." People used to say, Mr. Warren finally admits, "what a wonderful father and daughter we were—they used to wipe their eyes. We were just like lovers—and all at once we were lovers." [23] Nicole's insanity and cure are the main subjects of this plot, her reliance on and her eventual disentanglement from Diver. He is the psychiatrist-husband from whose craft and solemn care she must be weaned if, like Maggie, she is to love. Diver says that "the silver cord is cut and the golden bowl is broken"; although Fitzgerald went to Ecclesiastes for the metaphors, I suspect he was thinking of James's novel. For the cord is cut when Rosemary is initiated by Diver and the bowl is broken when Nicole no longer needs a surrogate father–husband–psychiatrist.

This novel climaxed and clarified a whole group of ideas, and ought to have helped connect modern literature with its sources. Rosemary is little different from a girl in a story published in 1856: the mother is a vegetarian, a member of one of the many eccentric groups of the day—Sylvester Graham's, the free-love Oneida Community, or that in Modern Times, New York. She has reared her daughter in her image and the girl has never tasted meat. The hero decides that this quirkiness is absurd: "In Georgiana I had found all that I required in a wife . . . I had come to preach vegetarianism; I abandoned it for the sweeter task of freeing a beautiful girl from its abominable slavery." They elope and when they return the mother surprises the girl at table. "Mr. Mephis, have you married this girl?" "This morning, madame." "Then you have a right to give her meat if you like."[24] The only difference between his achievement and Diver's effect on Rosemary is in the matter of wedlock. And Nicole, herself, is in exaggerated form very much like the girl who in 1855 married her father's physician.

Fitzgerald did indeed understand that ripeness requires freedom and that ripeness and freedom sustain love. But he never really understood the conjunction between American fathers and daughters and American culture, between love and society. This lapse is, I think, the chief reason why the novel ceases to be interesting once the two women achieve freedom. Diver is cast off. He disappears because he is a man, like Fitzgerald himself, who cannot fulfilll himself or his professional promise. Like Frederic Henry, Diver was born to love. Hemingway could say that the war destroys everything and thereby justify Henry's profound failure. Fitzgerald wanted to say something more perceptive but two facts of his own life got in his way: his marriage and the stillbirth of his career. He was shocked by society's behavior, by the inhumane war; boom and bust, vulgarity in art, degradations in politics and morality. This society, he felt, bred by a lovely dream of honor, is corrupt. The most powerful citizens, the very rich, are the most powerfully corrupt. In order to recover innocence, they send society's most noble men to Vienna where these men are supposed to learn the language of love. They are turned into gadgeteers and their services are bought by the corrupted rich. For society has no use for lovers and only, as Nicole's sister says, for psychiatrists—for the tinkerers, so Fitzgerald believed, with innocence and freedom.

Tender Is the Night, then, almost despite itself very nearly succeeded. Fitzgerald chose two old, parallel plots, added the international theme, introduced his own technical information about emotional disorder, and wrote a novel that accounted for the past while it dramatized the present. However, he could not isolate his own situation from Diver's and therefore he did not make his condemnation of society the final fulfilling aim of his novel. Instead, he decided for a paraphrase of the old homily: in Europe the wages of sin is perversion; in America, death. Fitzgerald—like Faulkner—is both an inventive and a traditional novelist. Until recently, our sense of the continuity of American letters relied almost exclusively on their work. Today, other writers—Robert Penn Warren, Wright Morris, Saul Bellow—have undertaken to exploit some of the best qualities of the past, to recover history not to bury it. Because Warren's impulse is at this time most fully realized, his fiction provides us with a clear illustration of this concern, some achievements and many possibilities.

Reinhold Niebuhr's phrase, the self and the dramas of history, expresses very precisely indeed Warren's main concern, his discovery of exactly what Thomas Mann saw in myth: a way of linking conscious and unconscious thought, past and present, the quick and the dead, great and small. This conviction has led Warren to conceive a new literary form, the serious historical novel in which national legends and myths unify a whole reading public in a coherent response to a given work. Warren's esthetic may or may not have special value for a new generation of writers who will address a new audience not of women merely, but of large numbers of people who have had a university education and who recognize some of the charms of high art. But it has allowed him to conceive five novels which recapitulate the whole spectrum of attitudes that shape the literature of love, to remold these attitudes to suit our current needs. Unlike most of his colleagues but very much in the fashion of his predecessors, he places the matter of love at the center not merely the margin of human experience. In *Night Rider*, for example, Mr. Munn's befuddlement and defeat by what Warren called "The World"—the arena of politics and economics—is expressed by an inner conflict and dramatized by his love for the two traditional kinds of women. This man of reflection who chooses the life of action must also choose between these women. A man as poorly equipped to live the life of passion as Reverend

Westlock was in *The Story of a Country Town*, he can hardly help being a blunderer.

Another kind of opacity ruins the people in *At Heaven's Gate*, a novel written toward the end of the time when the literature of social protest and class warfare was popular. It is, however, closer in spirit to Malraux's work than to Steinbeck's. For the novel attributes social disorder to various kinds of mythomania, to the taste for illusions, in the men who control society. In *Night Rider*, Warren caused Mr. Munn to commit himself to a public cause in part because this man wants to take on the job of reform and in part because he wants to escape a dull wife. What was there vaguely called "The World" in this novel is defined and embodied in the person of Bogan Murdock, a brokerage-house president whose corruption stems out of an "emptiness of the self." He has exchanged private emptiness for those forms of public vacancy commonly called Business, Industry, Government. Society itself, Warren believed, is a kind of conspiracy of scared people who lose themselves in the world of affairs in order to avoid self-confrontation. Thus Mr. Munn, unmanned by sexual uncertainty, cannot tell that he is lost, that his idea has been corrupted. But the people who do the corrupting are themselves illusionists and therefore are able most guilefully to shape the illusions which best perpetuate the conspiracy. They are, too, the people to whom society gives its highest rewards. Thus Murdock's deftness, the result of inner vacuity, is a symptom of what James would have called a waste of life — of an absolute inability to love. And this inability — the form his corruption takes — is signified in the classic manner, dramatized as his effect on his daughter. In the fashion of nineteenth-century financier-fathers — the manner established by a vast array of fathers in magazine fiction, by James's Sloper, Howells's Squire Gaylord, men who deprive their daughters of the proper kinds of affection — Murdock's own ruin and his daughter's are inextricable. Simultaneously, she is a girl of the thirties, a poor little rich girl who has been bred to be docile and proper but who discovers that Daddy is bad, love is good. And she sets about trying to compose a new life which would negate the old. Like Isabel Archer, she fails because she does not learn quickly enough to distinguish between sham and the real thing, between a mythomaniac poet and a heroic union-organizer.

The most famed work, *All the King's Men*, concerns the life of a man like Mr. Munn, but a man incapable of exercising choice in a world where only evil men have power. His immobility is conceived as a mode of escape, however, and not as the best response of a man of virtue. Jack Burden lacks virtue precisely because he lacks courage; without courage, he has no honor; without honor, he is capable only of selling his talents. And, Warren says, the reason why he has neither great courage nor high talent is not that he is mean but that he cannot love. Instead he is able only to idolize — Anne Stanton — or to ravish — Lois — and gain what Kinsey calls outlets. "I regarded Lois as a beautiful, juicy, soft, vibrant sweet-smelling machine for provoking and satisfying the appetite." Anne, however, like Roxy or Cressy or many other heroines in the genteel heartland, doesn't want ravishment or idolatry, and she knows that Burden, when we first meet him, is paralyzed. She longs for a man who would combine Willie Stark's vigor with her father's dignity, Willie's fire with patriarchal honor and responsibility. "Love isn't . . . like jumping off a cliff. Or getting drowned. It's . . . a way to live." Anne's virtue is not corrupted when she takes Willie as a lover; rather, her vigor is assured, and we recognize in her a woman who shows how men may live — she leads herself and her society to salvation by taking her man into her bed. This decision, then, guarantees her worth as a sexual partner and her reliability as an heiress of all the ages. Burden, too, eventually chooses a parallel American mode — he goes West and is reborn. "For that is where you come, after you have crossed oceans . . . after you have built cabins and cities and bridged rivers . . . composed resonant documents . . . and bathed your arms in blood . . . That is where you come, to lie alone . . . in a hotel room in Long Beach, California . . . I lay there . . . drowned in West . . . on the sea floor of History."[25] What he learns, in the matter of politics, is that he cannot accept either Willie's view or Adam Stanton's view because neither was complete. If in the name of God or the name of Science men of virtue — the Scholarly Attorney or

Adam Stanton — try to remain undefiled by removing themselves from the great arena itself, society has no choice but to elect Willie Stark. Confronting himself, out West, Burden finally sheds his masks, shakes paralysis, accepts the burden of Sisyphus. And he is ready to marry Anne Stanton whom now he loves neither as a kind of mother, Faulkner's Lena, nor as a kind of whore, Temple Drake.

Burden must revisit the past, must come to know Cass Mastern, must steep himself in History before he can know himself. But Jeremiah Beaumont in *World Enough and Time* is in fact a figure out of history, a hero of a historical novel, Warren's first. Warren chose this form, I think, mainly because he hoped it would make credible Beaumont's incredible hunger for sainthood, his tumultuous search for "innocence." And Warren felt that it was best, therefore, to return to the time when Puritanic Christianity controlled men's lives, to the time when pride described man's rejection of God. Warren calls pride man's rejection of man — that is to say, Beaumont's rejection of his wife. "I would conquer her . . . as Theseus took the Amazon . . . and I would expiate all ravage by becoming not her master but her most devoted slave."

But this is the inverted humility of a mythomaniac lover, of a man like Adam Stanton who carries around in his head an idea of what the world should be like. Its effect is to enslave this woman of high station who lives as a recluse because it is publicly known that she's had an illegitimate child. The child itself, much like Hester's Pearl in Hawthorne's novel, signifies her capacity to take the whole assault of life, to give herself absolutely. Beaumont does not recognize that this mine would yield a treasure — for we must also recall Warren's ironic use of James's idea — and instead he lusts after perfection. In consequence, he denies Rachel's physical lure, controverts her impulse to commit herself wholly to the natural world. And she dies, mad, clutching a half-breed's filthy infant in a cabin on the frontier. There, too, Beaumont is killed by enemies who despise his pose, his factitiousness, his playing at love as if it were a game of chess involving a glittering queen and a bad king and a gentle knight. For such people, Warren says, the frontier presents too heady a draft of reality, of nature itself, and it can bring no rebirth, only death. Before Beaumont dies, however, he recognizes in his passion for innocence what Hawthorne called the unpardonable sin: it does not represent a pure heart but a heart more corroded than any other. It is the "crime of self, the crime of life. The Crime is I." The kind of purity he had longed for is "what men cannot endure and be men"; on the contrary, "man must use the means of the natural world, and its dark ways, to gain that end he deems holy." [26] At the center of the natural world is the experience of human love. But its force can only destroy two people whose training has taught them how to die for each other but not, absurdly, how to live for each other and for themselves. Reanimating the principles of humanism inherent in the literature of love while at the same time criticizing, very severely indeed, the genteel code itself, he has tried to show how men can live without despair and, if they must, without God, and surely without nausea. And his latest novel, *Band of Angels*, is perhaps the first of what may become a series of efforts to realize these ideas in fiction which actually reconcile past and present, the world and the idea, the flesh and the spirit.

The story concerns the life and loves of a Southern slave girl, Amantha Starr, from 1844 to the beginning of this century. Amantha is not an ordinary slave for she is the daughter of a planter; her mother died, apparently in childbirth, and she thinks of herself as little Manty, the apple of her father's eye, his only daughter. When she is nine, he sends her to Oberlin where she is taught to abominate slavery and love God. At her father's death, which is timed to coincide with her puberty, she returns to Kentucky. Suddenly she is seized as property, sold to pay her father's debts. And now, for the first time, she learns that her mother had been Starr's slave. Amantha, beautiful and apparently white, is half-Negro. "Oh, who am I?" are the words with which the story opens, followed a moment later with "If I could only be free . . ." And these define her condition and her quest: moral freedom, Warren says at the outset, hinges on one's knowing who one is. Sold to a New Orleans man in whom kindness is a disease—that is to say, an enlightened slaveholder whose very enlightenment is invidious because it deprives his people of the will to be free — Amantha gives herself to him in gratitude. She hopes, too, that giving herself to her protector will help her discover what love is, and love, in turn, will help her to achieve a freedom more actual than mere manumission could accomplish.

This effort fails but failure teaches her something important, and it carries her to a second stage. For she learns that though freedom is indeed contingent on self-definition — she knows who she is — it requires, too, a capacity for love, a positive giving. Having made this discovery, she is ready to try marriage. Hamish, her owner, had made her feel "safe" but when she marries a Union captain, a New Englander of rich and profound liberal conviction, she discovers that she is deeply unsure of herself and of her husband's love. If Hamish were here, she thinks when she meets another of his former slaves, "I might be safe, might be protected from something." What she wishes to be protected from is nothing less than freedom itself for freedom is real, Warren says, only when it is based in self-acceptance. She does not yet realize that she cannot accept her blackness: "You mean . . . you can't stand being a nigger?" In her mind "nigger" signifies both social, legal disqualification and the taint of passion. Her marriage protects her against society. What horrifies her is the awareness that she is desirable because men react to the lure of blackness. This is indeed bitter medicine for "Dear Miss Sugar-and-Spice," reared at Starrwood and trained at Oberlin to be a household goddess. She cannot imagine herself as the ideal colored wench, "high-juiced and sweet-smellin'." Sex involves a repudiation or, as she says, a denigration. Yet until she accepts "denigration" she cannot accept herself. Actually, the men, particularly Hamish, are quicker than she to value the human being: "I didn't want to make you feel filthy, I didn't want to make you a nigger, like you said."

I stress this theme because it holds the key to Amantha's character. But the novel also treats of the Civil War; employs the internationality of New Orleans, in order to contrast its casual morality with the strait virtue of pietistic Ohioans; invokes the idea of Western health — indeed, it is finally in Kansas that Amantha comes to accept herself. Thus it covers the old map of society quite as it chooses the old symbols. But the matter that makes the novel cohere, the issue with which it begins and the perception with which it closes, is not any of these. Rather it is that other crucial concern of nineteenth-century fiction, paternality and daughterhood. The question that is implicit throughout the novel is, Why did her father not assure her freedom? The question is raised only once, near the middle, and at that time Amantha refused to listen to the woman who could tell why, her father's mistress. Warren wants her to discover the answer for herself. Comprehension can occur only when it has been prepared for by suffering, confusion, terror — only after Amantha can accept her taint. First she must have and admit a very frightening idea: she must realize that her energies have been expended in a single fruitless effort. You cannot buy freedom with devoutness. "*Nobody can set you free*," she finally realizes, for nobody can teach you to respect yourself. Nobody can free you, she comes to understand, "*except yourself*." Loving a man, many men, countless men, will not free you. Until you can love without guilt, love is meaningless, and you cannot be freed of guilt until you accept yourself. The reason why she is unable to love herself is that she has been unable to harmonize whiteness with blackness. This incapacity, in turn, is a result of her sense that her father had rejected and betrayed her. But in the end she understands that it was "his very love for me which made my father leave me to be seized at his graveside. He had not been able to make the papers out . . . that would declare me less than what he had led me to believe I was, his true and devoted child," his Manty.

This is what Warren says. Like James he does not say that the father was too deep down in the daughter's heart to be easily disengaged. A paraphrase of Warren's idea would say something like this: Starr sired a daughter who, like all children, is half free and half slave. But he could not relieve her of the slavery of perpetual daughterhood because his affection was deep and organic, so deep indeed as to constitute a betrayal. He had once sold a slave down the river, Amantha says, because he was jealous of her affection for the man. Slavery is Warren's metaphor for childish and perpetual daughterhood: autonomy can result only when daughterhood is overcome, for freedom must be achieved. It is never merely granted.

Now we can understand what Warren means by the taint of blackness: it represents Amantha's sense of doom, her conviction that her father has condemned her to sexual and moral bondage. This sense provided her with a kind of justification for passivity, for dependence. It relieved her of the responsibility to be free and allowed her to abdicate, Warren insists that we understand, the prime duty of every human being. Passivity not sexual bondage is what really doomed her, a taint of the spirit more insidious than any discoloration of the flesh. Feeling that her father had betrayed her, suddenly she had felt—on that trip to New Orleans, that descent into slavery—"an access of hatred . . . With that hatred something seemed to be settled, something relieved." What was relieved was the will to independence.

Amantha's blackness, therefore, signifies not merely the physical taint of sex to which she must become reconciled before she can live but mainly the moral evil, hatred, which impels her to use sex as the method with which to betray the men who love her. Finally realizing that the device must boomerang, must also cause her to betray herself, she purges herself of childish hatred and guilt. Gaining what Paul Tillich calls the courage to be—the courage to accept oneself despite the fact that one feels unacceptable—she harmonizes blackness and whiteness. Only then does she achieve the capacity to love, not its surrogate, an impossible and insatiable wish to be loved for herself alone and not for her yellow hair. Understanding that she is not bound—betrayed—by her father, she redeems herself and her husband and she is ready to assume her duties as an heiress of all the ages. The last moments of the novel contain her response to her husband's remark, "poor little Manty." The phrase has been a kind of refrain, interjected as if to underscore Warren's intention. "Don't call me that," she replies, "don't ever call me poor little Manty again."[27] For a lady of color can be a woman of destiny too.

Thus Warren has tried to reactivate history, to bring past and present into a new form of coalescence in which the American moral imagination and American sexual imagination cannot contradict but must complement each other. Deciding that love in one or another of its many forms is the central issue in this whole undertaking, he returned to the time when society, to its discredit, insisted that some degrading illusions become public truths; when society stifled desire and human freedom. And he discovered that the genteel tradition supported a clear-minded literature which directed its audience to attend and respect the very values which, in our time, we have tried so hard to dignify; that the modes of gentility must not be confused with its perspicuous and hard-headed effort to resolve the paradoxes of love, to solve the riddles of freedom.

I do not imply that Warren's achievement places him among the most eminent of our writers. His accomplishment is of a high order. But the model he presents to other writers is even more important because it indicates that our literature is organic and continuous, not unauthentic or removed from the main line of culture. It is after all pointless for each new literary generation to feel that it has no past, no idiom, no public, nor a coherent society, nor masters. Those were Cooper's and Hawthorne's problems and are no longer ours.

♀

Conclusion

"The difficult task of discovering and diffusing the materials of the American tradition — many of them still buried — belongs for the most part to criticism; the artist will steep himself in the gathered light. In the end . . . he will discover a relationship with the many streams of native character and feeling. The single writer — the single production — will no longer stand solitary or aggressive but within a natural sequence."

LITERATURE has guided us through an intricate national morality. It has informed us in majority decisions and minority dissents. It has speculated about the nature of love, created an imagery and a symbolism that dramatize the questions, and embodied the whole complicated affair in the American Girl. It has led us to the villages on both sides of the Mississippi and returned us back across the great Ocean. Its language has been traditional, its scenery attractive, its people neighborly. Despite the complexity of its subject it is a homely literature — reliable because it is matter-of-fact, a little clumsy because it lacks skills for contrivance, sweet because it seems uncontrived. James is the only genius it produced. We must exclude the other great men of the day, Melville and Clemens — Melville because he wrote only one novel, *Pierre*, which attempted in part to raise and answer these questions; Clemens because he disregarded them. Hawthorne, who helped James to learn how an artist must use his imagination and to understand American conditions, excludes himself. He and Poe were aloof; they preferred recondite subjects and did not conceive plots that report the American experience itself. Poe, Melville, Hawthorne, Clemens chose literature for a classic purpose — to teach and to entertain — and for this purpose the matter of love was too much circumscribed. On one occasion, in an unpublished book called "Letters to the Earth," Clemens interested himself in this issue: "a lot of people here spend a lot of time pursuing something called sex, and they spend a lot more time dreaming about it, and then they invent a Heaven where no such thing exists!"[1] But the remark occurs in no particular context. James is, however, a truly great artificer because—like Joyce, who said that he would do his job through silence, cunning, and exile—he combined simplicity with cunning, homeliness with exile.

The literature of love in America began when a self-consciously new society earnestly sought to integrate its theology, morality, and history in a single scheme that did the work of religion but did not require the old paraphernalia—churches, priests, services. For, as T. C. Hall remarks in his *Religious Background of American Culture*, the Pilgrims were separatists, largely secular in bias and interest. They set about achieving still another step toward a final reformation of what was, in the New England mind, that most indecent of abominations, the Roman Church.[2] Tacit rather than doctrinal, it is signified by the Puritan conviction that marriage rather than celibacy is the approved state of man. Since Elizabeth's day, however, England had maintained two competing opinions of women. On the one hand, they were considered inferior; society invoked religious sanctions to keep them in their place. On the other hand, many people claimed that women were competent—at the beginning of the eighteenth century Defoe argued this view—and therefore ought to be independent.[3] In America the two attitudes were set in high relief: marriage, a civil rather than a sacramental affair, was impelled less by social or economic convenience than by love.

Later, religious sanctions were used in order to limit sexual expression and activity. We have almost no specific information on why this control, by the end of the eighteenth century, seemed necessary. In 1891, however, Charles Francis Adams studied records in Braintree and Groton, from 1751 to 1777, and discovered that among two hundred persons, sixty-six confessed to having had premarital intercourse.[4] Our fiction traces this activity to the influence of the French and the threat of a persuasive deism. In any event, by the beginning of the nineteenth century a secular system was established: it invoked the authority of traditional religion in order to contain the passions of men and redirect these along new channels. The system placed women above men in the ladder of love, turned artists into lay preachers, and by 1850 it had succeeded so well that the falling birth rate caused learned men to wonder whether passion was failing or fertility declining.

But this scheme could not outlast the very old disagreement about the nature of love, nor could it overcome the Miltonic hope that man would some day forget his fears of hell and rephrase his hope of heaven. In the new land humanity hoped for a fresh start. Americans looked backward to Europe and forward to the frontier; urged restraint and admired vigor and freedom; idealized angels but married the neighbor girl because she was strong and pretty. And as their taste for practical solutions to even the subtlest perplexities were reinforced by science, the new sociologists and psychologists began to argue that "science proved" human passion to be moral and healthy. We read in the *American Journal of Sociology*, during its second year of publication, that Jesus recognizes the "physical basis of marriage" and "never regards it as in any way sinful or ignoble."[5] G. Stanley Hall's investigations express this interest as does the absurd but representative report, published in Hall's journal, which described a man's record of nocturnal emissions. It reported eight years of study and was designed to comfort people who conceive "emissions and the sexual or erotic dreams that commonly accompany them" as a sign of depravity. But, he said, "all unmarried masturbators and the married incontinent" must be warned: the "physiological limit" was 3.43 emissions each month.[6] Recalling Kinsey's data, we wonder if there really were giants in the earth in those days.

During the first half of the nineteenth century, literature preached the effects of the divine measuring rod, as Harriet Beecher Stowe believed, of angelic women. This state of mind could have caused a stalemate in our letters. Writers, despite public lore and discipline, became strikingly inventive and lucid. And the best among them never wholly committed themselves to the madonna's service. In a very muted but totally convincing way, our writers turned the notions of idolatry into a profound literature of love in which the whole aspiration of society was contained within and manifested by the character of the heroine.

The idea that women incarnated the meaning of a whole culture was indeed unique in history. Victorian England held similar views on sex, on wifely and motherly duties, on manliness. Victorian girls shared with American girls a common dilemma in which desire for a woman's reward, martyrdom, competed with a secret wish for sexual fulfillment. Thackeray, like James, could "treat the devious ways of the libido" with "penetration and consistency." "You never loved me, never—and were jealous of me from the time I sat on my father's knee," Beatrix tells her mother in *Henry Esmond*.[7] But Thackeray does not connect her inner life with the life of society—he does not identify Woman and Britain. Neither the great Queen Elizabeth nor Spenser's Una—and surely not Miss Liberty—replaced Saint George. But the American girl embodied her society—writers were never allowed to forget this fact—and literature was forced to examine the mechanisms of both in order to understand either. What succeeded mere idolatry, what James turned into literature of the very best kind, is the belief that unidealized love is the prime force in history; that this force had been purified and intensified in the New World. And though the concept was Christian and familiar, Americans were the first to create a national literature which recognized that the discontents of civilization were somehow implicated in the bewilderments of love.

I have insisted, perhaps too fervently, that we regard American heroines as embodiments of certain ideas. My fervor does not distort the tone of our writing, for in that supposedly leisured time literature was surely more strident than bland, more intense than assured. Like Emerson, Thoreau, Whitman, it moralized; it adopted the oratorical mode of old sermons. And like the heroines it admired, its intensity was of the brain, not of the blood. Yet, as

European audiences realized, American girls were neither bloodless nor shapeless.

But it is a real achievement of fiction that the heroine seems to live in four dimensions. This is partly a result of society's insistence that nothing be overlooked, nothing relevant be lost; the girl must be understood and her character must occur out of demonstrable causes. This discipline allowed writers to deepen her appeal even though they were accustomed to describe her physical appearance only in order to identify her motives or intimate her latent desires. Yet they created a woman who has weight, height, and proportion even though they said very little about her surface. Aside from the specific images of hair and flowers, occasional references to her figure, a writer masked his physical response to her sheer beauty behind his opinion of her spirit. Nevertheless, it is in fact her very reality, the sense she gives of having been simply removed from a garden party in Tuxedo Park, that literature evoked.

Perhaps because writers were supposed to evoke a bodiless response, the illustrators of the day were so highly prized. For the drawings of Gibson or Howard Chandler Christy turned an imagined but palpable person into an actual woman who appealed to the senses. These show fine-featured, shapely girls who stand tall, alert, regal. But their dark eyes show concern, even anxiety. Watching a tennis match at Newport or ascending the steps into the United States Hotel in Saratoga, they are remote, stately, troubled. The leading image, so popular in illustrations for novels, is that of a girl descending from a carriage. Her hat suggests her chic, and the simplicity of her long gown—exaggerating what the writers of the day called her *embonpoint*—assures her innocence. The lids of her eyes are neither open nor closed because she is neither bold nor prim. But she too is remote. Surely this handsome woman has no reason to adopt a pose so unsuited to our free and friendly society. Unless, perhaps, she requires remoteness as a kind of armor against the man, her devoted servant, whose arm she touches so very lightly. She seems to dislike him—"as though, in her womanhood," Anthony Trollope remarked, "the neighborhood of men was the same as that of dogs or cats."[8] But the man has done nothing: we know this because his moustache is sedate, his shoulders are narrow, his ankles are thin. He is a gentleman, obviously he has money, and doubtless she will marry him. But we realize that they will not be particularly happy. They will get on.

Unlike Trollope, most Europeans envied this man because they fancied that he was loved by a woman of the first order. They were unaware that her hauteur — what James called the great I AM of American women — was not a spur but a bar to love. An "Infinite Haughtiness" first fashioned her, Melville says of Mrs. Glendinning in *Pierre*, and the manners of gentility finished her. A woman of this kind knows only how to be a "devoted" wife and mother, as Mrs. Wharton said, an angel in the house. The problem, as James conceived it in *The Bostonians*, would not be solved when women were "emancipated." It would be solved only when women were actually free. And freedom is a moral achievement, not a legal victory.

The girl looks troubled, therefore, because she feels enslaved. And yet devotedness is what men admired: in part because they valued this quality so highly, fiction is preoccupied with daughters trained by fathers to be passionate but docile wives. This process, Howells believed, created charming children but not lively, independent women. James in the international plot showed how devotedness deprived them of the capacity for freedom. Thus Maggie is unhappy until she realizes that she must be independent and whole before she can experience love. Genteel fiction, then, began with idolatry, discerned that a new respect for sex must occur before men and women can love, perceived that American society bred troubled women who struck for freedom and gave the mere appearance of autonomy. And literature shaped a new myth based in an old dream of harmony and freedom. That ancient dream is best represented by a dream of love, it said. The force which calls into play yet disciplines human passion is love of woman. Understand a woman, therefore, and you comprehend the new order: "it was a virgin who bore the Savior; a woman to whom he, as a child, was subject, and by whom . . . he was trained and educated; to a woman . . . he gave the first clear proclamation of messiahship.

His first miracle was wrought because of the faith and at the solicitation of his mother . . . A woman was first at the tomb, the first to see the risen Christ."[9] A generation later, Sherwood Anderson — quite unaware that he invoked the very dogma he had rebelled against — was to say, "The Woman. Mystery. Love of women . . . What are they like? Are they like trees? How much can a woman thrust into the mystery of life, think, feel? Love men?"[10] These questions animated the myth of gentility, and literature itself embodies the answers on which society at large agreed. If you want to know the forces that create men, children, and culture, you must first know the secret of a woman's force. Her secret is the clue to the secret of love and her love, the source of life itself, is the best definition of the quality of being itself. Fiction portrayed the process through which a woman gains sexual competence yet retains honor, a process which must be understood if a man is to learn how to gain freedom, experience love, fulfill himself and the destiny of his nation. Led by James, literature declared that it was no longer on the side of the angels, dedicated itself to the cause of man. And a line of thought that developed after love had become secularized found its way to a stirring humanism.

But when the sexual revolution occurred, the American dream of love lost its enchantment; the American myth lost its cogency. What had been muted and private yet coherent in the genteel tradition did not achieve a new kind of coalescence when culture and literature came of age. Society leaped ahead and writers thought that the millenium had arrived, that the new triumph of infidelity would finally reconcile society's unconscious life with its public life, that the new freedom would be won when old constraints were overcome. Love, they discovered — totally unaware that their doctrine was hardly new or even dramatic — is "a strange, subtle coalescence of wonder and disgust. The beauty of love is the triumph of adoration over nausea."[11] When passion came of age, therefore, "idealism" was lost; when idealism went, somehow history and intelligence went too. And nausea came into being. Following nausea, today we have terror. And now, as in 1840 — as if the time between 1880 and 1910 had never been — our arts are too often deprived of real men and women. For instead of exploiting imagination to penetrate reality, our writers mask reality with a world of make-believe peopled by motherly or viperine or good-bad girls—enslaved women admired by slavish men.

There have been two notable efforts to counteract this situation. The first is that preached by the apostles of the organization state, who mistake "group-thinkometry" for mind and "togetherness" for love. They hope to reanimate by fiat the American dream. Hence we buy that issue of *Life* in order to learn about "Woman, Love and God"—to learn what sixty years ago was called Christian Sociology. "If woman . . . has one role more important than her others, it is the one symbolized by Mary as the source of love. Only as women guard the art and guide the quest of love can mankind know all the kinds and heights of love of which they are capable. The art and the quest begin in the family and end at God's feet." [12]

This is a most ambitious quest. Contemporary literature, however, is a little more worldly. And its activity constitutes the second main effort to confront the dilemmas of love. Our best writers undertake a deliberate invasion of the American past in order to remold its matter in ways which suit our sensibility and discourse. They help us to seize the ideas which the literature of love inherits from all the ages: moral freedom underlies human virtue but virtue is not its own reward, merely the ground of personal humaneness and national self-realization. Warren, Morris, Bellow adapt old myths to the modern situation, myths shaped by the genteel tradition in American letters. And until we recognize what its accomplishments were, we will be unable to gauge the quality of their work or that of others who will follow. Instead, we will hear our critics say, as Leslie Fiedler said recently, that "love in one guise or another remains the theme" of the European novel; but the American novel "demands neither husbands nor lovers—it does not even demand women!" Written virtually the other day, this remark carries the flavor of the twenties, that dead end where his essay, "From Clarissa to Temple Drake," does in fact stop. James's Daisy, we are told, could not marry, only die "and reborn, she became the fallen Daisy of Scott Fitzgerald's *Gatsby*, the heiress of all the ages turned real bitch." Beyond this Daisy "there is only Faulkner's Temple Drake, the final avatar of the Female Saviour in America, a drunk and a nymphomaniac."[13] Fiedler is brilliant but wrong. And though I report the ideas in his essay, what I'm referring to is a mode of thought to which most men of letters in America still subscribe. Our writing, they say, is concerned only with the failures of love in a society where passionless and emasculated men admire—according to their mood—only angels or vipers.

Reappraising this attitude and the literature on which it is based, we learn that American writing is strewn with the corpses of men and women who could not resolve the paradoxes or transcend the tensions of love. The dead are not victorious. The triumph goes to all the lustrous young women who combine magnetism and prudery, to the phalanx of anonymous writers who taught the old master-alchemist himself, James, how to mix the elements which make up Maggie Verver. And beyond Temple Drake there are Anne Stanton and Amantha Starr. They lead us not into evil but deliver us by showing that the way to salvation is through the door that Kafka feared to enter, that Malraux's Kyo allowed May to open for him and anyone else, that Bloom and Molly open for Dedalus. Unlike the European literature of love, however, American writing has identified women with society and suffused both with the messianic idea. As they themselves learn how to live, so they show us how to shed our innocence and if we do not respond the fault is ours not theirs. Once we assume the burdens of love, our literature says, we must also assume the obligations imposed by history and remold this nation in order that it will lead the way for all mankind.

When at last we overcome innocence and nausea,[14] we will discover that two girls died in Rome—Daisy Miller and Temple Drake.

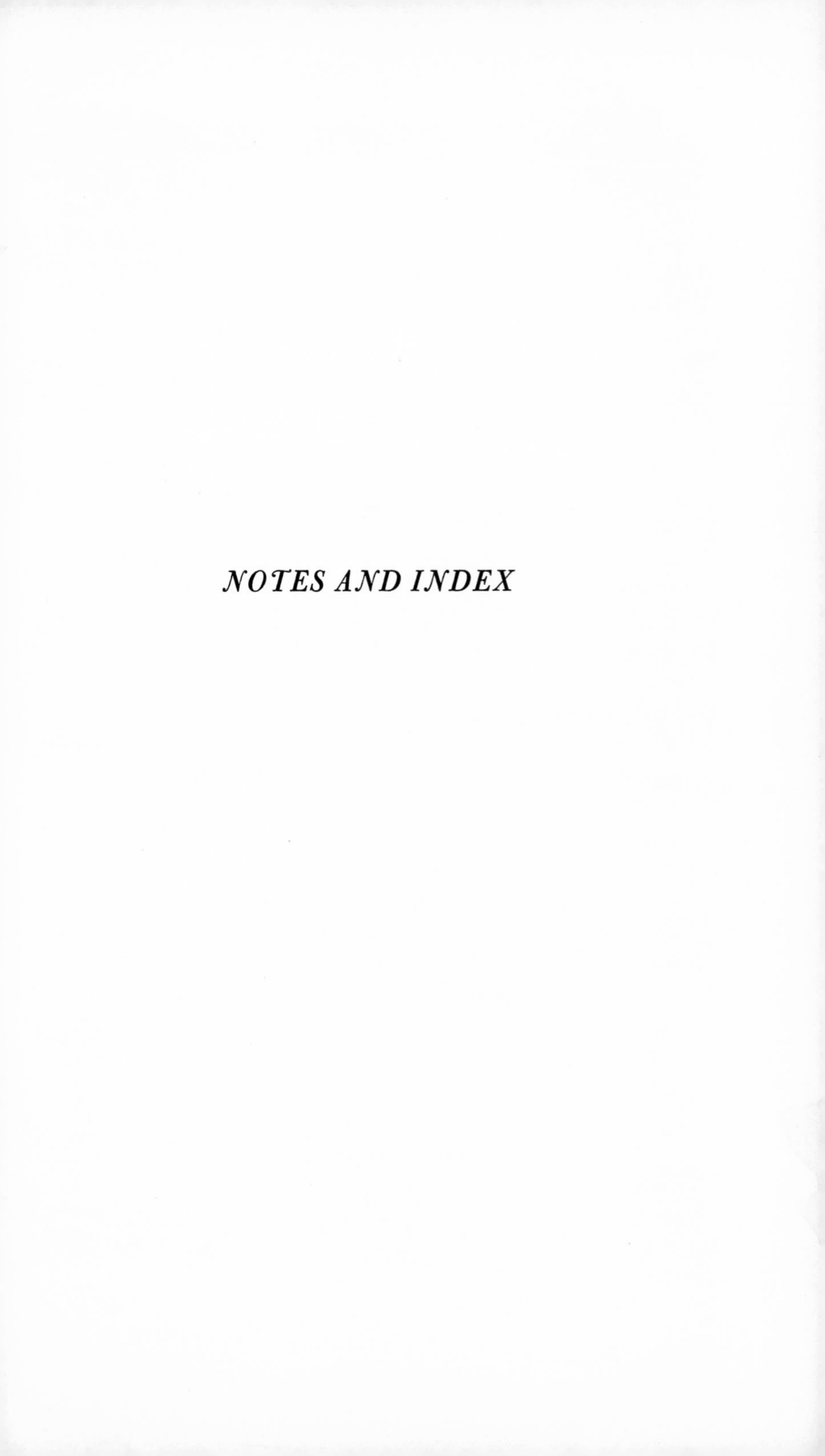

NOTES AND INDEX

♀

Notes

Steel-Engraving Ladies and Gibson Girls

EPIGRAPH: Robert Wayne, *The New York Times Book Review,* August 2, 1953, 3.

[1] L. Lewis and H. S. Smith, *Oscar Wilde Discovers America: 1882* (New York, 1936), 153. This opinion is widespread — Van Wyck Brooks and George Santayana are among its most famous adherents — and continues to mold criticism and social history. "Because women were the rulers of the home and home was where the novel was read, fiction came more and more to concern itself with women and their special world . . ." James D. Hart, *The Popular Book* (New York, 1953), 90. However accurate this attitude is in general, its effect has been to discourage inquiry into this special world.

[2] James Bryce, *The American Commonwealth* (3rd ed.; New York, 1940), 681.

[3] Thomas Beer, *The Mauve Decade* (New York, 1926), 53. Mr. Beer drew on many kinds of testimony but relied far too trustingly on information provided by such people as Edward Bok, editor of *The Ladies' Home Journal,* who have their own axes to grind. Bok, for example, bragged how he tamed Mark Twain, made him presentable to polite letters, mainly in order to take credit for establishing the reputation of a major writer (*The Autobiography of Edward Bok* (New York, 1921), 383–384).

[4] F. L. Pattee, *The Feminine Fifties* (New York, 1940), 93.

[5] Anne H. Wharton, *Salons Colonial and Republican* (Philadelphia, 1900), 156.

[6] A. W. Calhoun, *A Social History of the American Family* (Cleveland, 1917), I, 86–87.

[7] Frances Wright, *Views of Society and Manners in America* (London, 1821), II, 180.

[8] Captain Marryat, *Diary in America* (London, 1839), II, 1.

[9] Frances Trollope, *Domestic Manners of the Americans* (London, 1832), II, 180.

[10] "Our Wives," *Harper's Magazine,* XVII (November, 1858), 783–788.

[11] "Wanted, A Healthy Wife," *Harper's Magazine,* XIII (June, 1856), 75–83. See also A. L. Reed, "Female Delicacy in the Sixties," *Century,* XC (October, 1915), 855–864. William Dean Howells, ordinarily circumspect, remarked that American society "seems little better than a hospital for invalid women" (*Suburban Sketches* (Boston, 1872), 96).

[12] "The Social Condition of Women," *North American Review*, XLII (April 1836), 489–513.

[13] S. E. Morison and H. S. Commager, *The Growth of the American Republic* (New York, 1942), I, 474. In this matter of cultural history, I have drawn on the usual sources and have relied chiefly on the following: Merle Curti, *The Growth of American Thought*, New York, 1943; Louis M. Hacker and B. B. Kendrick, *The United States Since 1865*, New York, 1932; Matthew Josephson, *The Robber Barons*, New York, 1937; Stewart H. Holbrook, *The Age of the Moguls*, New York, 1953; Lloyd Morris, *Postscript to Yesterday*, New York, 1947; Allan Nevins, *The Emergence of Modern America, 1865–1878*, New York, 1927; Arthur M. Schlesinger, *The Rise of the City: 1878–1898*, New York, 1933; D. C. Seitz, *The Dreadful Decade . . . 1869–1879*, New York, 1926; G. M. Towle, *American Society*, Boston, 1870; F. J. Turner, *The Frontier in American History*, New York, 1920; J. P. Wood, *Magazines in the United States*, New York, 1949; Thomas W. Woody, *A History of Women's Education in the United States*, New York and Lancaster, 1929; Dixon Wecter, *The Saga of American Society*, New York, 1937.

[14] Eleanor Wolf Thompson, *Education for Ladies: 1830–1860* (New York, 1947), 135–136.

[15] But a generation later, when women were certain of their competence and employment, they resented discrimination of this sort. "In the same school where I taught, a man . . . commanded . . . double . . . because he was — a man . . . I neither wish to vote nor preach nor practise medicine or law," merely, despite bad syntax, "to be respected in my work" (Susan P. King, "My Debut," *Harper's Magazine*, XXVII (July, 1868), 531–532).

[16] C. J. Furness, *The Genteel Female* (New York, 1927), 235–236. See also Ruth E. Finley, *The Lady of Godey's*, New York, 1931.

[17] "A Woman's Poem," *Harper's Magazine*, XVIII (February, 1859), 340.

[18] "The Health of Our Girls," *Atlantic Monthly*, IX (June, 1862), 722–731.

[19] Christopher Crowfield, "House and Home Papers," *Atlantic Monthly*, XIII (March, 1864), 353–363.

[20] "Our Daughters," *Harper's Magazine*, XVI (December, 1857), 72–77. Later when the new social scientists investigated these matters, they "proved" that antifeminists were wrong. Radcliffe students, one researcher discovered, suffer no special "nervous condition" during the school year or during the period of examinations ("Effect of Study for Examinations on the Nervous and Mental Condition of Female Students," *Psychological Review*, V (January, 1898), 55–62).

[21] R. P. Utter and G. B. Needham, *Pamela's Daughters* (New York, 1936), 396.

[22] *Harper's Magazine*, XVI (March, 1858), 519–522.

[23] "Our Husbands," *Harper's Magazine*, XVII (September, 1858), 489–494.

[24] This was by far the most popular of genteel notions: "the best love" is one that "ripens long after the bloom of beauty and the lust of strength have languished" (*Ibid.*, 490).

[25] "Our Wives," 787.

[26] "Editor's Drawer," *Harper's Magazine*, XI (August, 1855), 423–424.

[27] *American Journal of Psychology*, III (November, 1890), 258–259.

[28] *Dr. Chase's Recipes* (Ann Arbor, 1867), 210.

[29] Mary Boykin Chestnut, *A Diary from Dixie*, ed. by Ben Ames Williams (Boston, 1949), 84. The use of opium was common but surreptitious and little discussed in public. It appears often in recipe books — the handbooks on homebrewed medicine — and occasionally in fiction. In one story, for example, a child dies because its gadabout mother learns too late that the nursemaid fed it laudanum instead of food ("A Mother's Confession," *Harper's Magazine*, XVII (July, 1858), 85–95).

[30] Chestnut, *Dixie*, 79.

[31] Emanie Sachs, *The Terrible Siren* (New York, 1928), 223–224.

[32] *Ibid.*, 79.

[33] Caroline Ticknor, "The Steel-Engraving Lady and the Gibson Girl," *Atlantic Monthly*, LXXXVIII (July, 1901), 105–108. I have chosen this version of the familiar contrast because it is one of the more dramatic. See also K. G. Wells, "Transitional American Woman," *Atlantic Monthly*, XLVI (December, 1880), 817–823; "Two Types of Women," *Lippincott's*, VI (March, 1893), 475–478; A. W. Warner, "The New Woman and the Old," *Century*, XLVII (November, 1909), 89–92.

[34] E. C. Lapham, "Woman's Duty to Woman," *Forum*, I (July, 1886), 455–467. From the post–Civil War period until beyond the turn of the century, spokesmen for this opinion believed that a society which disregarded their views was going literally to the devil. Their last resort and highest authority was Goethe. See E. W. Farnham, "Woman and Her Era," *Atlantic Monthly*, XIV (September, 1864), 389; E. W. Brodhead, "The Eternal Feminine," *Century*, XXXVII (March, 1900), 761–767; Newell Dunbar, "*Das Ewigweibliche* (The Ever Womanly, A Homily in Dialogue)," *The Arena*, XXXI (January, 1904), 180–198; Frank N. Hagar, *The American Family*, New York, 1905; Harriet Anderson, "Woman," *Atlantic Monthly*, CX (August, 1912), 177–183.

[35] *Julia Newberry's Diary*, ed. by M. A. Barnes and J. A. Fairbank (New York, 1933), 12.

[36] "An American Girl," *Scribner's Monthly*, XXI (December, 1880), 296–297.

[37] Mark Sullivan, *Our Times* (New York, 1927), II, 195. See also F. D. Downey, *Portrait of an Era as Drawn by Charles Dana Gibson*, New York, 1936.

[38] Antonio Marro, "The Influence of Puberal Development upon the Moral Character of Children of both Sexes," *American Journal of Sociology*, V (September, 1899), 193–219.

[39] Lester Ward, "Genius and Woman's Intuition," *Forum*, IX (June, 1890), 401–408.

[40] Charles F. Thwing, "What Becomes of College Women," *North American Review*, CLXI (November, 1895), 546–553. The debate on the nubility of college women, on the proper mode of conduct and activity for girls with higher education, was a leading concern of society from the moment when the women's colleges opened their doors. See A. Carlier, *Marriage in the United States*, New York, 1867; A. C. Brackett, "A Liberal Education for Women," *Harper's Magazine*, LIV (April, 1877), 695–696; J. H. Brown, "To Marry or Not to Marry," *Forum*, VI (December, 1889), 432–442; H. Starrett, "Future of Our Daughters," *Forum*, X (October, 1890), 185–196; F. M. Abbot, "College Women and Matrimony Again," *Century*, LI (March, 1896), 796–798; T. Bentzon, "Family Life in America," *Forum*, XXI (March, 1896), 1–20; T. Blanc, *Condition of Women in United States*, New York,

1905; S. L. Arnold, "The Education of Girls," *New England Magazine*, XXXVI (March, 1907), 81–84; Lydia K. Commander, *The American Idea*, New York, 1907.

[41] Albert Jay Nock, *Memoirs of a Superfluous Man* (New York, 1943), 226.

[42] C. W. Porter, "Physical Hindrances to Teaching Girls," *Forum*, XII (September, 1891), 41–49.

[43] Earl Barnes, "The Feminizing of Culture," *Atlantic Monthly*, CIX (June, 1912), 770–796.

[44] Esmé Wingfield-Stratford, *The Victorian Sunset* (London, 1932), 221–222. See also M. R. F. Gilman, "American and English Home Life," *Outlook*, LIX (May, 1898), 174–175.

[45] James Muirhead, *The Land of Contrasts* (New York, 1898), 53. See also Jacques Offenbach, *Offenbach in America*, New York, 1877; S. C. de Soissons, *A Parisian in America*, Boston, 1896; Hugo Münsterberg, *American Traits*, Cambridge, 1901.

[46] Paul Bourget, *Outre-Mer* (New York, 1898), 109. I have offered the barest sample of apostrophe in an age when people, discussing American women, seemed to suspend intelligence. One other instance is perhaps more than enough: American writers say, we are asked to believe, that they "find all about them all they need for a portrayal of one worthy to be the mother of the Divine Child" ("Some Modern Types of Mother," *Munsey's*, IX (November, 1893), 477–487).

The Antipodes of Love

EPIGRAPH: Gilbert Seldes, *The Movies Come from America* (New York, 1937), 35.

[1] James D. Hart, *The Popular Book* (New York, 1950), 86. Mr. Hart's is by far the most astute as well as the most original of a number of histories of American fiction. Cf. Edward Wagenknecht, *Cavalcade of the American Novel* (New York, 1952), 84–85.

[2] Alexander Cowie, *The Rise of the American Novel* (New York, 1948), 415.

[3] Timothy Dwight, *The Duty of Americans in the Present Crisis* (New Haven, 1798), 20–21. Nearly a century after Dwight's speech, similar prejudices were offered in condemnation of the whole feminist movement itself: "The Spirit of Unrest, released in the . . . French Revolution . . . laid his disturbing hand on Woman" (Ellen Desart, "Woman," *Eclectic Magazine*, LXVI (September, 1897), 377–382).

[4] J. F. Cooper, *Wing and Wing* (New York, 1860), 476–478.

[5] In the 1830's "it had been possible for a Lady to be coarse of speech and vulgar in manner . . . but from the '40's onward . . . she cultivated an evasive reticence of speech and thought" (C. W. Cunnington, *Feminine Attitudes in the Nineteenth Century* (New York, 1936), 107). For a lucid display of these and related changes — of the transmutation of women into ladies and then into an ineffable force — see C. Cushing, "Social Condition of Our Women," *North American Review*, XLII (April, 1836), 513–515; J. Agnew, "Women's Offices and Influence," *Harper's Magazine*, III (October, 1851), 655–657; H. Morford, "Womanhood and Chivalry in America," *Lippincott's*, I (April, 1868), 417–421; "Editor's Table," *Godey's Lady's*

Book, LXXXIV (July, 1872), 573; E. Lynn Linton, "Are Good Women Characterless?" *Forum*, VI (February, 1889), 644–652; Richard Harding Davis, "The Origin of a Type of American Girl," *Monthly Illustrator*, III–IV (January, 1895), 3–8; W. I. Thomas, "The Sexual Element in Sensibility," *Psychological Review*, XI (January, 1904), 61–67; William Graham Sumner, "The Family and Social Change," *American Journal of Sociology*, XIV (March, 1909), 577–591; Lyman Abbot, "Assault on Womanhood," *Outlook*, XCI (April, 1909), 784–788; Mrs. Burton Harrison, *Recollections Grave and Gay*, New York, 1911; Harry Thurston Peck, *Twenty Years of the Republic: 1885–1905*, New York, 1911.

[6] "Water Cure," *Harper's Magazine*, XI (June, 1955), 95–112.

[7] "My Wife," *Harper's Magazine*, XIX (August, 1859), 337–343.

[8] D. T. Kilbourn, "Revealings of a Heart," *Graham's Magazine*, XXXVI (January, 1850), 69–75.

[9] "Elkanah Brewster's Temptation," *Atlantic Monthly*, IV (December, 1859), 710–721.

[10] "A Modern Cinderella," *Atlantic Monthly*, VI (October, 1860), 435–441.

[11] "God and man had entrusted to women the high office of softening man's rougher instincts and ennobling his character" (Herbert Ross Brown, *The Sentimental Novel in America 1789–1860* (Durham, 1940), 106).

[12] This mystique maintains its power almost into the present time: "The Genteel Female is the most tangible symbol of one mysterious force that shapes our national character and destiny and makes of modern American life a unique experiment in culture" (C. J. Furness, *The Genteel Female* (New York, 1931), xlv). See also Hart, *The Popular Book*, 85.

[13] N. C. Iron, "The Maid of Esopus; or the Trials and Triumphs of the Revolution," cited in Edmund Pearson, *Dime Novels* (Boston, 1929), 62–63.

[14] Kate Putnam Osgood, "My Lady Leopard," *Harper's Magazine*, XLV (September, 1872), 592–598. See also D. R. Castleton, "The Little Heiress," *Harper's Magazine*, XXVII (September, 1863), 664–675; Jane Thorneypine, "A Dangerous Woman," *Harper's Magazine*, XXXII (April, 1866), 616–627. These stories seem to express what Freud called "a terror of castration," for the young men clearly feel threatened by and decide to flee sexual temptation ("Medusa's Head," *Collected Papers* (London, 1950), v, 105–106).

[15] "Our Husbands," *Harper's Magazine*, XVII (September, 1858), 489–494.

[16] Henry Giles, "Sentimentalism," *Harper's Magazine*, XXI (July, 1860), 203–211.

[17] In "Ligeia" we see Poe's awareness of the two opposing themes in American art and culture which Philip Rahv has named "Paleface and Redskin," *The Kenyon Review*, VI (Summer, 1939), 251–255.

[18] James G. Muirhead, *The Land of Contrasts* (New York, 1898), 53.

[19] "First and Last Love," *Harper's Magazine*, XI (October, 1855), 653–658. See also J. R. Chandler, "The Belle of the Opera," *Graham's Magazine*, XXXIV (January, 1849), 1–7; "The Third Bowl," *Harper's Magazine*, XI (August, 1855), 373–376; "Love and Skates," *Atlantic Monthly*, IX (February, 1862), 223–240; "A Woman," *Atlantic Monthly*, X (December, 1862), 694–707.

[20] The differences among generations are beautifully shown in the remarks of a girl living in Canandaigua, New York, and keeping a diary, 1852 until 1873, from her ninth to her thirtieth years. "Father sent us 'Gulliver's Travels' and there is a gilt picture . . . of a giant with legs astride and

little Lilliputians standing underneath . . . Grandmother . . . pasted a piece of pink calico over it, so we could only see the giant from the waist up" (Caroline Cowles Richards, *Village Life in America* (New York, 1914), 12). A few years later, the tone of amused forbearance is even more patent: "Bessie Seymour wore a . . . gold chain . . . and I told Grandmother that I wanted one just like it. She said that outward adornments were not of as much value as inward graces and the ornament of a meek and quiet spirit . . . I know it is very becoming to Grandmother and she wears it all the time but I wish I had a gold chain." (*Ibid.*, 62.)

[21] M. E. W. Sherwood, "New England Women," *Atlantic Monthly*, XLII (August, 1878), 230–237. This notion was widely held as a fact of nature, European as well as American, because it seemed to reach deep down to the core of national and personal character, seemed to explain national or private disaster. "Women hold a different position in the . . . sensuous and warm-blooded Southern countries from that . . . in the less erotic North." And this law applied no less accurately in 1888, we learn, than it had during the middle ages in Italy when "neither the matron's girdle nor the nun's capulary could restrain passions hot as the sun which gave them birth—deadly as the plague by which they were scourged" (E. Lynn Linton, "Italian Women in the Middle Ages," *The Fortnightly Review*, XLIII (1888), 252–272).

[22] Helen W. Pierson, "My Heart and I," *Harper's Magazine*, XXVII (August, 1863), 351–360. "Thirty years ago, an acute foreign critic remarked, apropos of a novel by Mr. Howells, that our novelists seemed to regard the Civil War as an occurrence that separated lovers, not as something that ought normally to have colored men's whole thoughts on life" (Van Wyck Brooks, "The Splinter of Ice," *The Seven Arts*, I (January, 1917), 277).

[23] Nora Perry, "Margaret Freyer's Heart," *Harper's Magazine*, XXVII (July, 1863), 179–189.

[24] F. O. Matthiessen and Kenneth Murdock, *The Notebooks of Henry James* (New York, 1947), 47.

[25] Henry James, *The Bostonians* (New York, 1872), 6, 5, 49, 2, 328.

[26] "We should know," wrote the reviewer of a new novel, that its author, "Christian Reid was a lady because all the men in the book are ladies or . . . ladies' men and are . . . much better or worse than they could be." And he warned young men not to "think of taking the lady novelists" seriously ("Reviews and Literary Notices," *Atlantic Monthly*, XXVI (December, 1870), 762).

[27] "Is it too much to hope that there is some man now living who will see American women freed from their slavery to French fashions?" (H. A. Delille, "American Women and French Fashions," *Harper's Magazine*, XXXV (June, 1867), 118–120).

[28] Robert Tomes, "Women's Form," *Harper's Magazine*, XXXVII (July, 1868), 202–208.

[29] Louise Chandler Moulton, "A New England Tragedy," *Harper's Magazine*, XXXII (January, 1866), 220–223.

[30] Harriet P. Spofford, "The Beautiful Miss Vavasour," *Harper's Magazine*, XLVI (May, 1873), 852–858.

[31] E. W. Olney, "One Too Many," *Atlantic Monthly*, XLII (August, 1878), 129–149.

[32] Hamlin Garland, *A Son of the Middle Border* (New York, 1914), 383.

The Lily and the Prairie Flower

EPIGRAPH: Alistair Cooke, *One Man's America* (New York, 1952), 218.

[1] Stewart H. Holbrook, *Yankee Exodus* (New York, 1950), 155.

[2] Louise Hall Tharp, *The Peabody Sisters of Salem* (Boston, 1950), 77.

[3] H. W. Lanier, ed., *The Best Stories of Mary E. Wilkins* (New York, 1927), 44–45.

[4] "Our Daughters," *Harper's Magazine*, XVI (December 1857), 76.

[5] A. W. Calhoun, *A Social History of the American Family* (Cleveland, 1917), II, 104. It wasn't long before farming became as genteel an occupation as any other: "This lady, so energetic and spirited . . . in out of door matters is, in the drawing room, the most gentle . . . retiring . . . modest of her sex" ("Woman on the Farm," *Harper's Magazine*, XXIX (August, 1864), 355–358).

[6] Henry Nash Smith, *Virgin Land* (Cambridge, 1950), 74.

[7] *Ibid.*, 119.

[8] Gertrude Atherton, *A Whirl Asunder* (New York, 1895), 14. Miss Atherton, apparently, based her heroines on live models — a fact attested by the description reprinted from *The San Francisco Chronicle*: "There is a wild flavor about the Californian which stamps her at once. She dresses a little louder and talks a little louder than other American women; she pays less attention to conventionalities and has less repose . . . She has a good deal of the California hardness." ("California Women," *Current Literature*, V (July, 1888), 27.)

[9] Frank Norris, *Moran of the Lady Letty* (New York, 1898), 230, 287, 325.

[10] Frank Norris, *The Octopus* (Garden City, 1949), I, 160.

[11] Henry James, *The Portrait of a Lady* (Boston, 1881), I, 129, 131. James used this subject in many stories, most patently in "A Siege of London" which was presumably based on Victoria Woodhull's character and experience. And though not all writers admired Western women, everyone agreed that these girls were especially vigorous, that their quality could be traced to geography and climate. Vital women were of course highly prized in a society that bred numberless invalids and I suppose this explains why a Western girl's health or adaptability is always noted. Richard Harding Davis, for example, remarked that only in the West could you find women who "adapt themselves as gracefully to snowshoes at Fort Bradley as to . . . giving dinners at Fort Houston" (*The West from a Car-Window* (New York, 1903), 205). A full-blown portrayal of this theme in fiction appears in Henry B. Fuller, *The Cliff-Dwellers*, New York, 1898; Robert Herrick, *His Great Adventure*, New York, 1913; Frank Norris, *A Man's Woman*, New York, 1899; William Dean Howells, *The Kentons*, New York, 1902; Edith Wharton, *The Buccaneers*, New York, 1938. The mass audience greeted these ideas, too, in one of the most famous novels of the day, Harold Bell Wright's *The Winning of Barbara Worth*, New York, 1910.

[12] H. H. Boyesen, "A Platonic Affair," *Harper's Magazine*, LXXX (February, 1890), 347–362. Cf. E. S. Phelps, "The Bend," *Harper's Magazine*, XXIX (August, 1864), 323–335.

[13] Henry Adams, *Esther* (New York, 1884), 46, 280.

[14] Edward Eggleston, *The Hoosier Schoolmaster* (New York, 1871), 111–112.

[15] Edward Eggleston, *Roxy* (New York, 1878), 291.

[16] *Ibid.*, 383.

[17] Edgar W. Howe, *The Story of a Country Town* (New York, 1927), 128, 330.

[18] Bret Harte, *Cressy* (New York, 1889), 43, 174, 189, 214, 221.

[19] Eggleston, *Roxy*, 30.

[20] William Vaughn Moody, *The Great Divide* (New York, 1910), 161, 138, 166. Another good and underprized writer concerned himself with similar matters: David Graham Phillips, *The Fashionable Adventures of Joshua Craig*, New York, 1909.

Fortune's Darlings

EPIGRAPH: Edward, Duke of Windsor, "A King's Story: Part II," *Life*, May 26, 1950, 63–86.

[1] Despite general agreement in the matter of national tone, the uniqueness of certain distinct types of women was constantly proclaimed. And a woman's spirit was usually attributed to the spirit of the place in which she originated. "The author of *An American Girl in London* was wise to choose Chicago as the home of her heroine. The Philadelphian would never have dreamed it possible to take such a journey alone. The New Yorker would have returned on the next steamer when her great aunt refused to receive her. The Baltimorean would have wept and resigned herself . . . while the Bostonian would have gone unchaperoned only as an art student . . . But the Chicagoan . . . having undertaken anything is pretty sure to go through with it." (M. J. Handy, "Women of the World's Fair City," *Munsey's*, VIII (March, 1893), 607–608.)

[2] Vance Thompson, "The American Social Invasion of Europe," *Munsey's*, XXXVIII (January, 1907), 545–548. Cf. Henry James, *The American Scene* (New York, 1907), 347–348.

[3] Thorstein Veblen, "The Barbarian Status of Women," *American Journal of Sociology*, IV (January, 1899), 503–514.

[4] August Carlier, *Marriage in the United States*, New York, 1867, cited in Dixon Wecter, *The Saga of American Society* (New York, 1937), 403.

[5] This most familiar of all themes in American fiction hardly requires much citation — any one story represents nearly all its clichés. See Lillian Bell, "Sir John and the American Girl," *Harper's Magazine*, CII (November, 1901), 955–962. Henry James collected most versions of this situation in *Lady Barbarina*, New York Edition, New York, 1908.

[6] It is this image which Alfred Kazin, speaking of Mary Martin's success in "South Pacific," invokes: "So sophisticated yet so natural, so independent and so obdurate in her search for the real thing . . . When Nurse Mary Martin, our fabulous American miss, truly fortune's darling . . . skips round and round in her delight . . . the audience knows that with no other people could war be such an occasion for the discovery of human sweetness, of love, of the most radiant happiness." ("We Who Sit in Darkness," *Commentary*, IX (June, 1950), 525–549.) A less literary statement and, perhaps, a more serious one occurred more recently in a newspaper story called "This Country's Best Ambassadors in Europe Are those Light-Hearted American Girls." We are asked to believe that our "American-garden-variety girl in a cotton dress and cardigan sweater" — "not Marilyn Monroe. Not Betty Grable, or Barbara Hutton" — "makes more friends than a dozen Marshall

Plans" because of her "fresh naturalness . . . her nice manners, her friendly good humor." (*The Philadelphia Evening Bulletin*, August 11, 1954, 1.)

[7] Fitz James O'Brien, "The Finishing School," *Harper's Magazine*, XVII (September, 1858), 434–447. See also "Marrying a Countess," *Harper's Magazine*, XI (November, 1855), 782–789; "Rachel," *Harper's Magazine*, XI (October, 1855), 682–687; "Countess Melusine," *Harper's Magazine*, XXII (April, 1861), 653–660.

[8] Wecter, *The Saga of American Society*, 408.

[9] The duty of an American husband and father, James said, is to keep her going. This woman's arrogance became, more and more, a matter for ridicule and eventually a cartoon depicted her languidly raising her arms up to the globe, disproportionately small, saying, "I want it." *Harper's Magazine*, XXVI (February, 1913), 486. See Mrs. Burton Harrison, *The Anglomaniacs*, New York, 1890; H. H. Boyesen, *Social Strugglers*, New York, 1898; W. D. Howells, *The Landlord at Lion's Head*, New York, 1897; Edgar Fawcett, *New York*, New York, 1898; Robert Herrick, *The Real World*, New York, 1901; Winston Churchill, *A Modern Chronicle*, New York, 1910.

[10] Edith Wharton, "The Last Asset," *The Hermit and the Wild Woman* (New York, 1908), 92.

[11] Edith Wharton, *The Custom of the Country* (New York, 1913), 21, 513.

[12] Edith Wharton, *The Age of Innocence* (New York, 1920), 366.

[13] Henry James, *The Wings of the Dove*, New York Edition (New York, 1909), ix.

[14] *Ibid.*, 439.

[15] *Julia Newberry's Diary*, ed. by M. A. Barnes and J. A. Fairbank (New York, 1933), 93, 76, 70, 149.

[16] William Dean Howells, *Heroines of Fiction* (New York, 1901), II, 176.

[17] Henry James, *Daisy Miller*, New York Edition (New York, 1909), 85–86.

[18] James's disclaimer convinced neither public, American nor European, but his analysis of Daisy's effect did indeed set the style of European writing on this theme. German writers, it is surprising to learn, decided that "Daisy Miller's coquetry goes so far only because it answers to no check of inner consciousness." And though her "physical and moral courage" was generally admired, "the American girl's purity . . . is not conceded." (Lida Von Korchow, "American Characters in German Novels," *Atlantic Monthly*, LXVIII (December, 1891), 824–838.)

[19] E. E. Bigelow, "An 'American Beauty'," *Century*, XXXIII (November, 1886), 207–214. Cf. Henry James, *Confidence* (Boston, 1888), 35.

[20] Edith Wharton, *Madame de Treymes* (New York, 1907), 35. Mrs. Wharton's attitudes had been anticipated in a story where protest was considerably more subdued. "What is this freshness [men] . . . laud? It is the crudeness which comes from inexperience." "How unlike American girls you are, Laura! You remind me of French women." (Nora Perry, "Laura and Her Hero," *Harper's Magazine*, XXIX (July, 1864), 169–179.)

[21] Henry James, *The Ambassadors* (New York, 1903), 104.

[22] This view was of course little publicized but did appear now and then. A girl was "Europeanized" in two ways: either she was subjected to more severe sexual discipline — the discipline of the *jeune fille* — or she was granted more freedom than was common at home. The heroine in a story by one of James's imitators, Constance Fenimore Woolson — herself an ex-

patriate who lived long in Italy — was considered beautiful and a perfect lady by Venetians but Americans thought her somehow "too — too — vigorous" ("In Venice," *Atlantic Monthly*, XLIX (April, 1882), 488–505).

[23] Henry James, *The Portrait of a Lady* (Boston, 1881), II, 434.

[24] Howells, *Heroines of Fiction*, II, 166.

[25] Oscar Cargill, "Medievalism of Henry Adams," *Essays in Honor of Carleton Brown* (New York, 1940), 329.

[26] "Types of Fair Women," *Munsey's*, XVII (June, 1897), 361–368.

The Spirit of Myrrha

EPIGRAPH: *The Philadelphia Evening Bulletin*, August 26, 1953, 27. Dante, *Inferno*, XXX.

[1] Western suspicion of new persons or ideas — an attitude which Turner disregarded — doubtless stems from the day when a frontiersman had to be trigger-happy in order to protect himself and his family. But this cast of mind lingers and today William S. White, writing on what he calls the midwestern Republican mind, observes "it is a mind . . . that is far quicker to suspect the worst in foreign nations or peoples than to presume the good or the best." Its habit, too, is to approach problems in much the fashion described by Eggleston and Howe — "either-or, this-or-else, black or white." Mr. White conceives these modes as modern but of course the lines of development are long. ("The 'Midwest Mind' in Congress," *The New York Times Magazine*, March 1, 1953, 10, 31.)

[2] Lionel Trilling, *The Opposing Self* (New York, 1955), 276.

[3] Henry James, *Partial Portraits* (London, 1888), 121–122.

[4] Louise Chandler Moulton, "A Wife's Story," *Harper's Magazine*, XXIV (December, 1861), 42–53. See also "A Girl's Dilemma," *Harper's Magazine*, XI (June, 1855), 86–91; "Hester Graham," *Harper's Magazine*, XVIII (February, 1859), 373–377. The characteristic situation is summarized by a remark in another story which refers to the heroine whose father has recently died; she's "an only child and no mother; there was probably a close tie between them" ("One Too Many," *Atlantic Monthly*, XLII (August, 1878), 129–149).

[5] Edgar Fawcett, *An Ambitious Woman* (Boston, 1884), 8.

[6] H. H. Boyesen, *The Light of Her Countenance* (New York, 1889), 91–92. Cf. F. Marion Crawford, *Adam Johnstone's Son*, New York, 1895.

[7] William Dean Howells, *An Open-Eyed Conspiracy* (New York, 1897), 87.

[8] *Dictionary of American Biography* (New York, 1929), I, 323. Cf. "Theodosia Burr," *Harper's Magazine*, XXIX (August, 1864), 293–305.

[9] Harold Dean Cater, *Henry Adams and His Friends* (Boston, 1947), Introduction, v.

[10] Ishbel Ross, *Proud Kate* (New York, 1953), 200.

[11] Henry Giles, "Margaret Fuller Ossoli," *Harper's Magazine*, XXIII (July, 1861), 220–229.

[12] "Our Queer Papa," *Harper's Magazine*, XVII (November, 1858), 789–796. The italics are the author's and seem at first glance to imply a pun. I am grateful to Walter W. Hamburger for clarification of this odd detail: "Actually this term [organic affection] was widely used in medicine during the same period, as a synonym for disease . . . probably neurosyphilis, though the spirochete was not isolated . . . until 1905." (letter from Dr.

Walter W. Hamburger, Associate Professor of Psychiatry, the University of Rochester School of Medicine and Dentistry, February 24, 1957).

[13] Nora Perry, "Rosalind Newcomb," *Harper's Magazine*, XX (May, 1860), 778–793.

[14] Thomas Bailey Aldrich, "Marjorie Daw," *Atlantic Monthly*, XXXI (April, 1873), 401–417.

[15] Nathaniel Hawthorne, *The Wonder-Book, Tanglewood Tales, Grandfather's Chair* (Cambridge, 1883), 55–74. There are some important similarities between Hawthorne's stories and two folk tales current during this period—"The Devil's Pretty Daughter" (c.1870) and "The Girl and the Road Agent" (c.1900)—connections which place this attachment throughout the whole range of American culture. The first story is a native adaptation of an old tale: the daughter and her lover outwit the rich father, called Devil, a man who had tried to discourage all suitors. The second is apparently American in origin. A moneylender amasses a fortune which he entrusts to his sixteen-year-old daughter who serves as the collector of his debts. Returning home one day after gathering that day's receipts, the girl is attacked by a road agent who is about to rape her when her money spills out of the bags. He stops to pick up the scattered cash and she leaps on his horse, rides off to discover that the agent's saddlebags are full of gold and silver. (Vance Randolph, *The Devil's Pretty Daughter and Other Ozark Folk Tales*, New York, 1955.)

[16] "The Beauty," *Harper's Magazine*, XI (July, 1855), 193–196. The motifs of this plot are neatly exposed in a story, "Millicent"—the heroine's name is itself a kind of personification—where the wrong-minded daughter of a money-mad father is discredited and dismissed as "the beauty, the impoverished heiress, the rejected bride" (*Harper's Magazine*, XIII (June, 1856), 67–75). Among the popular writers of the day, it was Frank Norris who was most alert to the connections between gold and lust. Indeed, *McTeague*, the famed study of degradation, is the most convincing of his novels precisely because he caused the two themes to crisscross, the imagery of the first reinforcing the tension of the second thereby enlarging the intensity of both. Trina's emotions, he says, "reduced themselves at last to but two, her passion for her money and her perverted love for her husband when he was brutal." From time to time, "a brusque access of cupidity" would seize her but she didn't turn to her husband. Instead she drew tighter "the strings of the little chamois-skin bag that she hid at the bottom of her trunk" and then she would "play with this money by the hour." "One evening she . . . spread all the gold pieces between the sheets, and . . . stripping herself, slept all night on the money, taking a strange and ecstatic pleasure in the touch of the smooth flat pieces the length of her entire body." (*McTeague* (New York, 1899), 194–195, 223, 225.)

[17] Justin McCarthy, "Caught by an Heiress," *Harper's Magazine*, XLIII (September, 1871), 596–601.

[18] Harold Frederic, *The Damnation of Theron Ware* (New York, 1896), 379, 135. Along with Frederic's work, we can include other fiction popular during the Gilded Age which links fathers and daughters and excludes mothers: Gertrude Atherton, *The Californians*, New York, 1898, and *Ancestors*, New York, 1907; Robert Herrick, *A Life for a Life*, New York, 1900. It was another novelist, however, Winston Churchill, who most accurately reproduced this situation in novels which had the widest publicity available in that day. Freud, remarking the conditions which create the

female oedipal situation, noted that when "conjugal love has grown cold, the child may be taken as a substitute for the love-object which has ceased to attract" (*A General Introduction to Psycho-Analysis* (New York, 1938), 184). Helene Deutsch confirmed this idea and added certain observations on the private fantasies of young women who find themselves thus chosen. The girl believes that "the father loves the mother as a sexual object, but gives his better self . . . to his daughter. She is the one, she thinks, who understands him and possesses his soul." (*The Psychology of Women* (New York, 1944), I, 201.) Combining Freud's remark with that of Miss Deutsch, we pretty well define the substance of Winston Churchill's plots. Victoria, he said in a characteristic novel, was her father's "right-hand man"; "he thought his daughter's judgment better than his wife's." Her mother "knew him as the fountainhead from which authority and money flowed, but Victoria . . . had been his refuge from care, and in the haven of her companionship he had lost himself for brief moments in his life. She was the one being he really loved." (*Mr. Crewe's Career* (New York, 1908), 299.) Discovering that Churchill penetrated and reproduced the fantasies of his readers, I suspect that we begin to account for his fame. Cf. *Life*, July 14, 1950, 13, where this interplay among psychoanalytic theory, popular literature and American social history occurs in still another remarkable instance.

[19] Sigmund Freud, *New Introductory Lectures in Psycho-Analysis* (New York, 1933), 162.

[20] Hamlin Garland, *Rose of Dutcher's Coolly* (New York, 1899), 104–105, 111, 112, 333.

[21] In Dreiser's day, Randolph Bourne, a critic of rare clarity and extraordinary courage of mind, best understood Carrie's special quality. "Dreiser has done a real service to the American imagination," Bourne wrote, in "going gravely to the business of picturing sex as it is lived in the personal relations of bungling, wistful, or masterful men and women." (*History of a Literary Radical* (New York, 1920), 199.)

Nymph and Nun

EPIGRAPH: Sigmund Freud, *A General Introduction to Psycho-Analysis* (New York, 1938), 292–293.

[1] Henry James, *The Spoils of Poynton*, New York Edition (New York, 1908), viii.

[2] William Dean Howells, *The Rise of Silas Lapham* (New York, 1948), 258, 367.

[3] William Dean Howells, *An Open-Eyed Conspiracy* (New York, 1897), 180.

[4] William Dean Howells, *A Woman's Reason* (New York, 1883), 14, 38.

[5] Howells, *Lapham*, 13.

[6] William Dean Howells, *A Modern Instance* (Boston, 1881), 102, 103, 503.

[7] Henry James, "The Marriages," *Atlantic Monthly*, LXVIII (August, 1891), 233–252.

[8] F. O. Matthiessen and Kenneth Murdock, *The Notebooks of Henry James* (New York, 1947), 91.

[9] Henry James, *The Golden Bowl*, New York Edition (New York, 1909), I, 122.

[10] F. O. Matthiessen, *Henry James: The Major Phase* (New York, 1944), 89.

[11] James, *The Golden Bowl*, I, 141, 150.

[12] *Ibid.*, I, 129.

[13] *Ibid.*, I, 12.

[14] *Ibid.*, I, 10, 16.

[15] *Ibid.*, I, 384.

[16] *Ibid.*, I, 156.

[17] *Ibid.*, I, 154.

[18] *Ibid.*, I, 187–188.

[19] *Ibid.*, I, 385.

[20] *Ibid.*, I, 223.

[21] *Ibid.*, II, 292–293.

[22] *Ibid.*, II, 135.

[23] *Ibid.*, II, 275.

[24] Logan Pearsall Smith describes how war fever caused an amazing *volte face* in this most sedate of men. Smith's anecdote reports James bursting into Edith Wharton's home saying, "My hands are dripping with blood . . . I have been bayoneting, my dear Edith, and hurling bombs and ravishing and raping [the Germans]" (Simon Nowell-Smith, *The Legend of the Master* (New York, 1948), 167).

Sugar and Spice

EPIGRAPH: Warner Fabian (Samuel Hopkins Adams), *Flaming Youth* (New York, 1923), 6.

[1] Philip Rahv, *Image and Idea* (Norfolk, 1949), 44.

[2] Peter Monro Jack, "The James Branch Cabell Period," *After the Genteel Tradition, American Writers since 1910*, ed. by Malcolm Cowley (New York, 1937), 143.

[3] Samuel D. Schmalhausen, "The Sexual Revolution." *Sex in Civilization*, ed. by V. F. Calverton and S. D. Schmalhausen (New York, 1929), 387.

[4] F. Scott Fitzgerald, *The Beautiful and Damned* (New York, 1922), 81. Fitzgerald had the imagination of disaster and this suited a time when revolt was at least as much fantasy as fact. The women he wrote about, we begin to realize, had not "changed their attitudes as completely as they thought, and in spite of lipservice to freedom and equality, they retained many of their bourgeois values" (Caroline Ware, *Greenwich Village 1920–1930* (Boston, 1935), 240). And today, as Kinsey's study indicates and as others have long been aware, "a woman may have any kind of sexual life that she wishes if, and only if, she does not make herself conspicuous" (Clara Thompson, "The Role of Women in This Culture," *A Study of Interpersonal Relations*, ed. by Patrick Mullahy (New York, 1949), 159).

[5] John W. Aldridge, *After the Lost Generation* (New York, 1951), 40.

[6] Max Lerner, speculating on this matter, mocked men who fear "that they may encounter some Texas Lilith or some Jersey Jezebel and be vanquished and sunk without a trace" ("Idle Thoughts on Leap Year," *New York Post*, February 29, 1956, 44).

[7] Aldridge, *Lost Generation*, 91.

[8] Lionel Trilling, "The World of Sherwood Anderson," *The New York Times Book Review*, November 9, 1947, 1.

[9] Martha Wolfenstein and Nathan Leites, *Movies: A Psychological Study* (Illinois, 1950), 41, 19.

[10] *Time*, August 23, 1948, 40.

[11] Lewis Jacobs, *The Rise of American Film* (New York, 1939), 535.

[12] Edgar Dale, *The Content of Motion Pictures* (New York, 1935), 108.

[13] Gilbert Seldes, *The Movies Come from America* (New York, 1937), 33.

[14] Carl Van Vechten, *Spider Boy* (New York, 1924), 272–273. The early 1920's provided many versions of similar women — Anna in Ben Hecht's *Eric Dorn*, New York, 1921; Virginia in Waldo Frank's *Holiday*, New York, 1923 — when writers began to express wonder at the idea that good and wifely women could be also women of passion. The best of the lot is Campaspe Lorillard in Van Vechten's *The Blind Bow-Boy*, New York, 1923. In the definitive scene, she lies in bed reading Pirandello, Aldous Huxley, Norman Douglas, Ronald Firbank — and *The Book of Common Prayer*. Heroines of this type seemed especially stirring, as Tallulah Bankhead in 1927 stirred Cecil Beaton, who called her a "wicked archangel" (Tallulah Bankhead, *Tallulah* (New York, 1952), 124).

[15] Booth Tarkington, *The Flirt* (New York, 1912), 291, 65.

[16] *The New York Times*, September 23, 1952, 102.

[17] Few critics make even a stab at understanding this affair. The reviewer of John O'Hara's *10 North Frederick*, for example, is one of the very few who have even recognized that an issue exists. "Between father and daughter there is that slightly incestuous love which is *de rigueur* in so many novels today . . . Ann, the daughter, is one of these beautiful, sad figures in flight from Daddy's arms into too many other arms" (Sidney Alexander, "Another Visit to O'Haraville," *The Reporter*, January 26, 1956, 44–47). Cf. William Styron, *Lie Down in Darkness*, New York, 1951.

[18] Stephen Spender, *World within World* (London, 1951), 194.

[19] W. M. Frohock, *The Novel of Violence in America, 1920–1950* (Texas, 1950), 204.

[20] *Time*, November 9, 1953, 87.

[21] *The New York Times Book Review*, December 2, 1951, 63.

[22] Arthur Mizener, *The Far Side of Paradise* (Cambridge, 1951), 240.

[23] F. Scott Fitzgerald, *Tender Is the Night* (New York, 1951), 18.

[24] "My Mission," *Harper's Magazine*, XIII (June, 1856), 54–58.

[25] Robert Penn Warren, *All the King's Men* (New York, 1946), 401, 399, 408.

[26] Robert Penn Warren, *World Enough and Time* (Garden City, 1951), 108, 458.

[27] Robert Penn Warren, *Band of Angels* (New York, 1955), 1, 270, 231, 363–364, 375. This matter of blackness and whiteness is another abiding theme in our literature, and an obsession among our people. Cf. Joseph Holt Ingraham, *The Quadroone*, New York, 1841; G. W. Cable, *The Grandissimes*, New York, 1880; Mark Twain, *The Tragedy of Pudd'nhead Wilson, and the Comedy of those Extraordinary Twins*, Hartford, 1894; Gertrude Atherton, *Senator North*, New York and London, 1900; Waldo Frank, *Holiday*, New York, 1923. During intermissions at dances held, in the 1930's, by students at the University of Alabama, a ritual was enacted in which "the lights are turned out and . . . men march in carrying flaming brands. At the end of the procession four acolytes attend a long cake of ice . . . Then the leader . . . lifts a glass cup of water and begins a toast . . . 'To Woman, lovely woman of the Southland, as pure and chaste as this sparkling

water, as cold as this gleaming ice, we lift this cup, and we pledge our hearts and our lives to the protection of her virtue and her chastity.' " (Carl Carmer, *Stars Fell on Alabama* (New York, 1934), 14–15). What Faulkner thought of this ideal and of the confusion it perpetrates, he allowed Temple Drake and Popeye, Miss Burden and Joe Christmas, to illustrate; what he thought of this "leader," he showed in Percy Grimm. The whole affair itself, however, has received very wide publicity as a result of a recent study of mental illness: C. H. Thigpen and H. M. Cleckley, *The Three Faces of Eve*, New York, 1957. "Two distinct personalities, Eve White and Eve Black, are warring against each other. Out of the conflict emerges a third personality calling herself Jane." (Joost M. Meerloo, *The New York Times Book Review*, March 24, 1957, 14). This is of course the conflict and resolution described in the literature of love during more than a hundred years.

Conclusion

EPIGRAPH: Constance Rourke, *American Humor* (New York, 1931), 302.

[1] "The Talk of the Town," *The New Yorker*, February 7, 1957, 25.

[2] T. C. Hall, *Religious Background of American Culture* (New York, 1930), 83 ff.

[3] Mary Sumner Benson, *Women in Eighteenth Century America* (New York, 1935), 102–103.

[4] George R. Stewart, *American Ways of Life* (New York, 1954), 186.

[5] Shailer Matthews, "Christian Sociology, The Family," *American Journal of Sociology*, I (January, 1896), 457–472.

[6] Anon., "Nocturnal Emissions," *American Journal of Psychology*, XV (January, 1904), 104–107.

[7] Howard O. Brogan, "Rachel Esmond and the Dilemma of the Victorian Ideal of Womanhood," *ELH*, XIII (June, 1946), 223–232.

[8] Anthony Trollope, *North America*, ed. by D. Smalley and B. A. Booth (New York, 1951), 200. William James in a letter to his sister Alice remarked and approved the unique American feminine style because it spurred men to ever higher achievement. Our "insolent" women, he said, who show an "ill-feigned contempt" for men, goad them to "desperate excursions of manliness." Ralph Barton Perry, *The Thought and Character of William James* (Cambridge, 1948), 110.

[9] Matthews, "Christian Sociology," 468.

[10] Sherwood Anderson, *Dark Laughter* (New York, 1925), 95.

[11] Samuel D. Schmalhausen, "The Sexual Revolution," *Sex in Civilization*, ed. by V. F. Calverton and S. D. Schmalhausen (New York, 1929), 402.

[12] "Woman, Love and God," *Life*, December 24, 1956, 36. Perhaps we should add another view, the Marxian, to this pair, for all three distort life and literature despite somewhat different angles of vision. "The 'good woman' in fiction is the woman happily confined in . . . 'her proper sphere.' *Love* not labor is a woman's concern and woman's place is in the home." (Margrit Reiner, "The Fictional American Woman," *Masses and Mainstream*, VI (June, 1952), 1–10.)

[13] Leslie A. Fiedler, "From Clarissa to Temple Drake," *Encounter*, VIII (March, 1957), 14–22.

[14] It is this impulse to overcome innocence and nausea which shapes Humbert Humbert's character and design in Vladimir Nabokov's prodigious

novel, *Lolita.* The girl herself is a classic American brat but she serves him in much the way, Nabokov says, Virginia Clemm served Poe: passion produces in Humbert "the teasing delirious feeling of teetering on the very brink of unearthly order and splendor." This feeling is identical with that evoked by virtually all American heroines of fiction. In this fiction, however, it is manifested in a nymphet; passion itself is portrayed as nympholepsy — a frenzied desire for the unattainable — the state of being in which the beastly and the beautiful merge. And these peculiarly American states of desire and of being are rendered cogent, at once strange and familiar, by the plot itself which is composed as a kind of "parody of incest." The novel is extraordinary, therefore, not in its purpose and subject and plot, but in the form of its discourse. For it is written in the rhetoric and idiom of a passion so intense and outrageous that we are compelled to enter a realm of experience where innocence is fey and disgust is gauche. (*Lolita* (New York, 1955), 232, 289.)

Index